Women's Voices

Women and Religion Series

Women Priests?   ED. ALYSON PEBERDY
After Eve   ED. JANET MARTIN SOSKICE

Women's Voices

Essays in
Contemporary Feminist Theology

EDITED BY
TERESA ELWES

Marshall Pickering
An Imprint of HarperCollins*Publishers*

Marshall Pickering is an Imprint of
HarperCollins*Religious*
Part of HarperCollins*Publishers*
77–85 Fulham Palace Road, London W6 8JB

First published in Great Britain
in 1992 by Marshall Pickering

1 3 5 7 9 10 8 6 4 2

230
.082
W873

A catalogue record for this book is
available from the British Library

ISBN 0 551 02572–7

Phototypeset by Intype, London

Printed and bound in Great Britain by
HarperCollins Manufacturing Glasgow

This volume is dedicated
to the sound of women's voices

CONTENTS

SERIES INTRODUCTION

Theology, writes the German theologian, J.-B. Metz, "must again and again be interrupted by praxis and experience. The important questions to be asked by theology, then, are: Who should do theology and where, in whose interest and for whom?"*

Women, one assumes, have always been religious, but women have not always written theology. Indeed, if one is considering theology as an academic discipline (certainly not the only definition) then women have only been admitted in any numbers to universities as students of theology since the Second World War.

A remarkable feature of the theological scene in recent years thus has been the steady increase of writings by women on religious matters, and writings about women in religious faith and life. Almost inevitably, many of these writings are by new pens and have appeared in journals of limited circulation. Yet it is sometimes at such edges and not from the heartlands that the faith grows. This series hopes to bring works of importance to wider audiences.

The Women and Religion series has as its broad brief to publish writings of religious importance by women and/or about the place of women in the world's faiths. Some of these writings may recognisably be formal theology, some may not, and some may challenge the distinction of what counts as theology and who is a theologian in the first place.

Dr Janet Martin Soskice
The Divinity School, Cambridge University

*J.-B. Metz, *Faith in History and Society* (London, Burns & Oates, 1980), p.58.

THE CONTRIBUTORS

Janet Martin Soskice lectures in the Faculty of Divinity at Cambridge University and is a Fellow of Jesus College. She is the author of *Metaphor and Religious Language* (OUP 1985), and editor of *After Eve: Women, Theology and the Christian Tradition* (Marshall Pickering 1990).

Jane Williams read Theology at Cambridge and did research on the theology of hope. She was a member of the British Council of Churches Commission on the Doctrine of the Trinity, and the Archbishop of Canterbury's Commission on the Episcopate.

Elizabeth Sarah has been involved in the Women's Movement for many years. She is co-editor with Dale Spender of *Learning to Lose* (Women's Press 1980, 1988), and with Scarlet Friedman of *On the Problem of Men* (Women's Press 1982) and editor of *Reassessments of First Wave Feminism* (Pergamon Press 1982). In 1984 she helped to found *Shifra: A Jewish Feminist Magazine* and commenced study for the Rabbinate. She was ordained in July 1989 and is minister of Buckhurst Hill Reform Synagogue in Essex. She is also a member of the Working Party on Women and Judaism within the Reform Synagogues of Great Britain.

Linda Woodhead is Lecturer in Christian Studies at the University of Lancaster. At the time that her contribution to this book was written she was Lecturer in Christian Doctrine and Ethics at Ripon College Cuddesdon. She is editor of *Studies in Christian Ethics* and is currently engaged in research on the religious thought of the Bengali poet Rabindranath Tagore.

Lynne Broughton is an Associate Lecturer in the Faculty of Divinity at Cambridge University and lectures in Christian Ethics at Lincoln Theological College. She has published articles on philosophy, theology, feminism and church architecture.

Sarah Coakley is Tutorial Fellow in Theology at Oriel College
Oxford and lectures on feminist theology in the Theology Faculty
at Oxford University. She was previously Senior Lecturer in
Religious Studies at Lancaster University. She is the author of
Christ Without Absolutes: A Study of the Christology of Ernst Troeltsch
(Oxford, OUP 1988), and has contributed chapters on prayer
and spirituality to the two most recent Church of England Doc-
trine Commission reports: *We Believe in God* (London, Church
House Publications 1987) and *We Believe in the Holy Spirit*
(London, CHP 1991). She is currently editing a book on religion
and the body (Cambridge, forthcoming).

Mary Grey is Professor of Feminism and Christianity at the
Catholic University of Nijmegen in The Netherlands. She is
author of *Redeeming the Dream: Feminism, Redemption and Christianity*
(SPCK, 1989) and a former President of the European Society
of Women in Theological Research.

Daphne Hampson holds doctorates in Modern History from
Oxford University and in Theology from Harvard University.
She has since 1977 been a Lecturer in Systematic Theology in
the Department of Divinity at St Andrews University. Dr Hampson was the first and founding President from 1986–88 of the
European Society of Women in Theological Research. The
author of many articles on feminist theology, her first book *Theology and Feminism* was published by Basil Blackwell in 1990.

Ursula King is Professor and Head of the Department of Theology and Religious Studies at the University of Bristol. She has
published books and articles on Teilhard de Chardin, modern
Hinduism, and women in world religions, notably her volume
Women and Spirituality: Voices of Protest and Promise (London, Macmillan, and New York, Amsterdam Books, 1989, 1993[2]).

Teresa Elwes is the editor of this volume. She is a final-year
undergraduate reading Theology and Psychology at St Edmund's
College, Cambridge. She is also a founder member of the Cambridge University Feminist Theology Group. Before coming up
to Cambridge she trained as a type designer, calligrapher and
letter cutter, working as a monumental mason for a number of
years.

EDITOR'S INTRODUCTION

The papers in this volume were first given at Cambridge University in 1990 and 1991 during the very popular open lecture series "Women's Voices in Religion". Although the invited speakers were asked to choose their own titles, the collection hangs together particularly well and expresses some of the major concerns of women in religion in Britain today.

As women the authors have the advantage that traditionally their sex has kept them on the boundary of theological and religious discourse. From this position their vision and insight can challenge theory without losing sight of reality. Here they weave together life experience and religious discourse and unite a readership of both academics and the general public.

The series emerged from the desire of a group of women undergraduates, the Cambridge University Feminist Theology Group, to hear more women theologians and to give feminist theology a platform in Cambridge. It was organised independently and on a shoe-string (we had no financial support when the speakers were invited). The success was exhilarating with the largest lecture hall in the School of Divinity packed for many sessions. People came from a wide variety of backgrounds and locations and after the lectures conversation continued with an open invitation to the pub and then to supper.

The ivory towers at last seemed to reverberate with women's voices in religion. Not only were the lectures successful but there is now in the Faculty of Divinity a lecture series on feminist theology, a weekly graduate seminar, and a less formal "women-space" group at the Von Hügel Institute, St Edmund's College that is open to all.

There has been considerable demand for the lectures in printed form. I am delighted that this has now become a reality.

It remains now for me to thank the many individuals and institutions that have made the series and the volume possible: Janet Martin Soskice for inspiration and support throughout; the

Von Hügel Institute for financial backing and hospitality for the speakers; St Edmund's College and St John's College for further financial help; Anna Petrie and G. A. Elwes for invaluable help with the preparation of this volume; Rebecca Williams for supporting me; Morna Hooker for introducing the series; the Faculty of Divinity for welcoming the initiative; and the lecturers, the participants, the readers and the Cambridge University Feminist Theology Group for the happening.

Teresa Elwes
St Edmund's College, Cambridge
October 1991

~ 1 ~

Can a Feminist Call God "Father"?

JANET MARTIN SOSKICE

Let me distinguish the question I wish to address in this paper from two others which don't directly concern me here. The first is the in fact misguided question of whether feminists must *always* call God "father". It is misguided because there's no basis, theological or philosophical, for insisting that the feminist or anyone else should use one divine title exclusively. God has always had many names in the Jewish and Christian traditions – One, rock, king, judge, vine-keeper – and will continue to do so. The second, not misguided, question is: "Is it expedient for feminists and those sympathetic to them to call God 'father' in writings, prayers and liturgies where continuing to use this title may mask an imbalance in our ideas about God?" This is an important question with practical and theoretical ramifications, but it is not the one I wish to consider here. My more radical question hovers around the question of expedience but is separable from it. It is this: "Can a feminist be at home in a religion where 'father' is a central divine title, if not necessarily in current usage, then certainly in the foundational texts and the subsequent history to which these have given rise?" Is the fatherhood language central to this religion and, if central, does it not bind Christianity fast to an unacceptable patriarchal religion which the feminist must reject? The question, "Can a feminist call God 'father'?" thus resolves into two others which are: "Can the

'father' language be eradicated from text and tradition?" and
"Can a feminist live with Christianity if it cannot be eradicated?"

So just what is in a name? What hangs or doesn't hang on a
particular notation? If we "designate" the same subject in a
different way are we saying anything different? Wittgenstein
struggled with these questions as he tried to escape from the
rigid and unworkable theory of language which he put forward
in his early work, the *Tractatus*. In the pages of the *Blue and Brown
Books* Wittgenstein becomes more sensitive than ever he was in
the earlier work to the ambiguities of natural language. He puz-
zles over the capacity of a notation to affect understanding and
even perception. He imagines someone who wants to divide
England differently from the customary divisions, who objects to
convention. "The *real* Devonshire is this," the objector says. But
he is answered, "What you want is only a new notation and by
a new notation no facts of geography are changed." But is this
really so? Does the new notation change nothing? "It is true,"
Wittgenstein adds, " . . . that we may be irresistibly attracted or
repelled by a notation."[1]

What difference does a new notation make? Why are we irresistibly drawn or repelled? Why does one metaphor or set of
metaphors seem to fit the situation exactly, and another not?
And what happens when a set of metaphors cease attracting and
begin to repel? In any religion where God is conceived of as
radically transcendent it is arguable that all the language used
of God will be metaphorical or at least figurative. This means
that a change in preferred metaphor or notation is always a
theoretical possibility and, indeed, Christian religious language
like that of any other religious tradition is a mobile thing, respon-
sive to the needs and perceptions of religious adherents. For the
most part, however, shifts in guiding metaphors take place slowly
and are largely unnoticed. Talk of the Christian as "slave of
Christ" or "slave of God" which enjoyed some popularity in the
Pauline Epistles and early Church is now scarcely used (despite
its biblical warrant) by contemporary Christians who have little
understanding for or sympathy with the institution of slavery
and the figures of speech it generates. The abandonment or
neglect of this metaphor was not forced, it just happened. Stu-

dents of the history of metaphor can see other metaphors wax and wane.

But at certain points in religious history one sees abrupt changes of imagery, a sudden revulsion from accustomed metaphors and preference for new or different ones. A dramatic instance today is the controversy surrounding the metaphor "God as Father". The immediate cause for complaint is the growing number of women (and men) who find sex-exclusive language in the liturgy and, by extension, the tradition's almost exclusively male language for God both alienating and offensive. Given the universal and egalitarian nature of Christian faith, they say, we can no longer say the Credal "for us men and for our salvation" or "Almighty and most merciful Father". This language must go.

At first glance this problem may appear open to a simple resolution. The churches could – like industry, government and other institutions – simply shift over to sex inclusive language (e.g. "for us and for our salvation") and complement the male images of God with a sprinkling of female images taken from Biblical text and tradition, for example Jesus' description of himself as a hen gathering her chicks or Anselm's address of Christ as "mother". This achieves an initial plausibility because on one fundamental point agreement can be reached by all concerned. It is this: God is not a human being and *a fortiori* not a male human being. God is not a male and God is not literally "father". For classical theologians, like Aquinas, "father", and "king" are metaphorical divine titles because they imply limitation. Aquinas restricts what can literally be said of God to a few, bare predicates – the so-called "perfection" terms: One, Being, Good, etc. These terms, which to his mind do not involve limitation, can be predicated literally of God, even though we may not know what their full significance would be in the Godhead. Aquinas, like most of Christian orthodoxy, would have difficulty with the idea that the naming of God as father is more than figurative speech. Indeed, the insistence that the God really "is" father occurs within Christian heresy. Certain Arians insisted that the Bible does not speak symbolically of God and thus that God *is* the Father and Christ *is* the Son. From this followed the heretical conclusion that the son, Christ, must have been non-existent before begotten. The consensus is then that calling God "father" is a metaphor, however central.

Now optimistic, or perhaps naive, egalitarian reformers seemed to suppose that to admit that all language about God is figurative would lead readily to the supplementation or even replacement of the male language of God-hood by female alternatives. But this easy resolution has proved unacceptable to conservatives and revisionists alike. Why so?

While it may be that, at the level of pure theological theory, God is not male, at the level of ideology God is or has been male in the Jewish and Christian religions. At this point we find unexpected agreement between religious conservatives and radical feminists – both agree that the God of Christianity is untransposably male – and it is for this reason that the conservatives insist that no change to the Church's language is possible, and that some feminists leave the churches and become "post-Christian" feminists.

The case for those, whether conservative or radical, who say the Christian God is untransposably male is a strong one. It is beyond doubt on a strictly textual basis that the stylisation of God in the Old Testament is as a masculine God and that the few feminine images of God (as a nursing mother or a nesting eagle) are always subservient to guiding masculine images. With the Christian New Testament comes the added force that Jesus' preferred title for God is "Father". Nowhere does Jesus invoke God in prayer except by this title. He teaches his disciples to pray "Our Father". Over and against feminist sensibilities then, seems set Dominical command. But what of those feminists who find they do not wish to abandon either Christian faith or feminist principles, who are convinced as Christians of the full dignity of men and women, and that the Christian message must be consonant with this dignity? Let us look more closely at our dilemma.

Putting things bluntly, as Mary Daly does, it is this: "If God is male, then male is God."[2] If God is seen as male then woman is not fully in the image of God. This conclusion is not a new one, in fact it was reached by a number of (male) theologians of the early Church – women are not fully in the image of God. Often cited in this context was 1 Corinthians 11:7 "For a man ought not to cover his head, since he is the image and glory of God; but woman is the glory of man", understood by some of the fathers to imply that women somewhere *were not* in the image of God. This conclusion, remote from most contemporary Christian intuitions, was reached by a combination of a certain sensitivity to the metaphorical nature of biblical texts, and a set of cultural assumptions about "female nature". The "Fathers" realised that the "image" in question was not a physical image, for God does not have a body. Rather, they concluded, it was by virtue of man's capacity for freedom, rationality and dominion that he was "in God's image". But these features – rationality, freedom and dominion – were precisely those which, according to the consensus of classical antiquity, women lacked. In a line that can be traced from Plato and Aristotle, right through Philo, Origen, Augustine and up to the debates surrounding women's suffrage of our own modern time, women have been held to be deficient in reason, and naturally subordinate, and the marriage relationship to be one of natural ruler to natural subject. It is not surprising that many of the "Fathers" thought women were not fully in the image of God. Chrysostom, at the turn of the fourth century says:

> Then why is the man said to be in the "image of God" and the woman not? Because "image" has rather to do with authority, and this only the man has; the woman has it no longer.[3]

Ambrosiaster, writing about the same time, reverses the normal order or argument which went from religious conviction to civic status by arguing from the civic status of women to conclusions about their religious status as "*imago Dei*":

> For how can it be said of woman that she is in the image of God when she is demonstrably subject to male dominion and has no authority? For she can neither teach nor be a witness in a court nor take an oath nor be a judge.[4]

By such circular reasoning women and other non-dominant groups have ever been kept in their places.

If God is styled as male, then the female is that which is "not God". Female titles are reserved in the Catholic tradition for the Church, the soul, Nature, and Mary.[5] Often the female is associated with negative features, or features which play a negative role in a set of balanced pairs. Thus in patristic literature a tendency emerges to characterise the female as carnal, emotional and creaturely, as opposed to the male which is spiritual, impassible and divine. In his allegorical interpretation of Genesis the Jewish neo-Platonist Philo says that the woman, Eve, represents the sense perception which leads the man Adam (who symbolises reason) to fall. Furthermore the supposed "natural" subordination of woman to man, as natural subject to natural ruler, was taken by many of the Fathers to be the paradigm of other kinds of divinely imposed subordination. So Chrysostom again:

> For since equality of honour does many times lead to fightings, He hath made many governments and forms of subjection; as that, for instance, of man and wife, that of son and father, that of old men and young, that of bond and free, that of ruler and ruled, that of master and disciple.[6]

It should be clear from this by no means exhaustive discussion that what disturbs feminist theologians is not simply that God has been styled as male in the tradition, but that God is styled as male in particular ways and especially has been styled as powerful, dominant, and implacable. This is the feminists' real objection to the rhetoric of patriarchy, not just that it subordinates women but that it also gives divine justification to a hierarchical reading of the world invariably conceived in terms of powerful/powerless, superior/inferior, active/passive, male/female. One is reminded of the anti-Calvinist remark of the Chevalier Ramsey, a Scottish contemporary of David Hume's:

> The grosser pagans contented themselves with divinising lust, incest, and adultery; but the predestinatian doctors have divinised cruelty, wrath, fury, vengeance, and all the blackest vices.[7]

It is this image of God as distant and controlling that the feminist theologian, Sallie McFague, finds so unsatisfactory. The primary metaphors in the tradition are hierarchical and dualistic. To speak of God as king, ruler, lord is to portray God as so omnipotent and other from God's creatures as to make reciprocity and love between God and humankind an impossibility. She suggests that even the one metaphor that might have permitted more mutuality, "God as father", has been compromised by its consistent association with omnipotence, as in "almighty Father".[8]

Here then, is the feminist objection – much broader than the simple objection that the language of Bible and Church excludes women, and reaching right into the "fatherland" of the Christian tradition. The mere complementing of male images with attendant female ones is clearly not enough. As Rosemary Ruether says, "We cannot simply add the 'mothering' to the 'fathering' of God, while preserving the same hierarchical patterns of male activity and female passivity. To vindicate the 'feminine' in this form is merely to make God the sanctioner of patriarchy in a new form."[9] Similarly, tinkering with the language of the liturgy, changing "he" to "he and she" may be a cosmetic change which conceals a more profound and, from the feminist's point of view, idolatrous tendency to pray to a male God. After Foucault and Ricoeur we can no longer think the interrelation of ideology and language so simple nor so easily unravelled.

There is little consensus, however, even amongst feminists as to whether how such problems should or even could be resolved. One might replace the "father/son" symbols with symbols from nature,[10] but this would diminish the personal element that others like McFague feel to be essential. One could speak of God as "Mother-Daughter-Spirit", but this language finds no home amongst the texts from which Christianity takes rise, and is perhaps also open to a hierarchical reading. One could speak, as Mary Daly prefers to, of God as "Be-ing" (Daly refuses now to use even the word "God"), but this abstract language runs the risk of making God even more remote, a tendency McFague deplores. Moreover it could be argued that any of these strategies, if employed not to complement but actually to replace

the Christian language of "God as father" would result in the
institution of a new religion, that the language of "fatherhood"
is too deeply rooted in the Christian texts and the religion itself
too intimately tied to those texts. The best course then for the
feminist who could not accept the language of "divine fatherhood" would be not to tinker with models of God but to abandon
Christianity, a step from which post-Christian feminists have not
shrunk. And as for feminists who find they cannot abandon
Christianity? Must we accept all the apparatus of patriarchal
religion if we accept the language of God's fatherhood? Is there
not another way, a way by which the language of divine fatherhood may be detached from the male idol of a patriarchal
religion? This is what I would like now to explore.

I am encouraged in this project by an article of Paul Ricoeur's:
"Fatherhood: From Phantasm to Symbol". One of his central
theses is that the "father figure is not a well-known figure whose
meaning is invariable and which we can pursue in its avatars,
its disappearance and return under diverse masks; it is a problematic figure, incomplete and in suspense. It is a *designation* that
is susceptible of traversing a diversity of semantic levels . . . "[11]
He applies his arguments to three fields: psychoanalysis (Freud),
the phenomenology of spirit (Hegel) and the philosophy of
religion. It is the treatment of this last that most concerns us
here.

In discussing the "Dialectic of Divine Fatherhood" Ricoeur
takes as his discussion partner not the theologian but the exegete.
He has interesting reasons for doing so. First, exegesis, as
opposed to theology, remains at the level of "religious representation" and does not carry the "refinements" of later theory.[12]
Exegesis, the study of the texts, is concerned with the progression
of representation in these texts and, in this case, with the development of the figure of the "father". Furthermore, exegesis "invites
us not to separate the figures of God from the forms of discourse
in which these figures occur".[13] The particular kind of discourse,
whether saga, myth, prophecy, hymn, or psalm is important
because the designation of God differs according to the manner
in which he is designated; whether God is described as agent, or
spoken on behalf of, or invoked in prayer.

Ricoeur draws attention to a remarkable aspect of the texts themselves – the qualitative insignificance of the divine title "father" in the Old Testament. Ricoeur's observation may be usefully complemented by some research by Robert Hamerton-Kelly who notes that whereas God is described as "father" over 170 times by Jesus in the New Testament, and never invoked in prayer by any other title, God is designated "father" only eleven times in the entire Old Testament and never invoked as such in prayer.[14] Instead, in the early narratives (or sagas) of the Book of Exodus, God is described as "the God of *our* fathers" (my emphasis). The connection certainly exists between God and patriarchy and with Israelite family life of this time, for just as families are headed by fathers, fathers are headed by leaders of clan or tribe who ultimately are responsible to God. But still it remains, God is not "father" but "God of our fathers" and the difference is significant. Hamerton-Kelly argues that this Mosaic strand in the Old Testament identifies "the God of our fathers" through the narrative and by means of historical association "rather than the mythological schemes of the Ancient Near East in which the gods are imagined to be the 'biological' fathers of human beings . . . Mosaicism replaces creation by a mythical procreation with creation by the mysterious Word of God . . . Fatherhood is strictly a symbol or metaphor for God's relationship to his people."[15] Ricoeur, too, speaks of the remarkable "reservation" on the part of the Hebrew people. The main name relation of God to the people in Exodus is covenant and not kinship – it is, at best, the adoption of Israel and not their biological generation by God. God is *not* described as "father", the people of Israel are *not* true "sons". The prime name of God in Exodus is that given to Moses from the burning bush, I AM THAT I AM, a connotation, Ricoeur says, without designation. Indeed it is a "name" that casts itself in the face of all names of God. In Exodus "the revelation of the name is the dissolution of all anthropomorphisms, of all figures and figurations, including that of the father. The name against the idol."[16] The God of Israel is defined, then, over and against father gods, gods who beget the world and, paradoxically, it is this abolition of the biological father God that makes non-idolatrous, metaphorical "father language" about God possible. By means of a number of other designations (liberator, lawgiver, the bearer of name without image) space is created where God may be called "father". Movement may then take place to the designation of God as father which takes place in the prophets, to declaration of the Father, and finally the invocation of God as Father complete only with the Lord's Prayer in the New Testament.[17]

The prophets are of particular importance to Ricoeur for, to his mind, they announce the exhaustion of Israel's history, and look to the future kingdom of God. It is here the father figure is declared and recognised, and it is a figure of futurity and hope, a hope for a relation that is to be. Ricoeur cites the extraordinary Jeremiah 3:19–20 where God speaks to his "faithless children" thus:

> . . . I thought you would call me, My Father, and would not turn from following me.
>
> Surely, as a faithless wife leaves her husband, so you have been faithless to me, O house of Israel.

In this "mutual contamination" of kinship metaphor, where God is both father and spouse to Israel, Ricoeur sees the "shell of literality" broken and the symbol liberated. "A father who is a spouse is no longer a progenitor (begetter), nor is he any more an enemy to his sons; love, solicitude, and pity carry him beyond domination and severity."[18] The father figure is not, as Ricoeur has insisted, an "invariable figure" but problematic, incomplete, even shocking.

Within the Christian writings that make up the New Testament a further shock occurs. The modest eleven designations of God as "father" in the Old Testament contrast sharply with the 170 times Jesus designates God as "father" in the very much shorter New Testament. Even more remarkable is the fact that Jesus uses the domestic title of "father", *Abba*, when invoking God. This title, *Abba*, in all probability is the designation used by Jesus himself. Moreover it would seem a designation central to his eschatology. Hamerton-Kelly says the "intimacy and accessibility of Almighty God is the essence of Jesus 'good news'.

God is not distant, aloof, not anti-human, not angry, sullen and withdrawn: God draws near, very near; God is with us."[19] Already then, we see the turning of the symbol, the God who is "not Father" in Exodus, becomes father and spouse in the prophetic literature and is revealed in the intimacy of the address of *Abba* in books of the New Testament.[20]

According to Ricoeur, the audacity of addressing God as *Abba* breaks the "reserve to which the whole Bible testifies . . . The audacity is possible because a new time has begun." And he goes on:

> Far, therefore, from the addressing of God as father being easy, along the lines of a relapse into archaism, it is rare, difficult, and audacious, because it is prophetic, directed towards fulfilment rather than toward origins. It does not look backward toward a great ancestor, but forward, in the direction of a new intimacy on the model of the knowledge of the son.[21]

On a Christian reading of the scriptural texts this movement from phantasm to symbol, the retreat from the language of physical generation to that of a word of designation (I AM THAT I AM) is completed by the audacious address of the Son. In Ricoeur's terms it is only with the true Son that one can have true Father, for "father" is a dependent title, "there is a father because there is a family, and not the reverse".[22] It is the Son as first-born amongst the children of God who, in this sense, makes God "father". And it is in the Son's death that this distinctive fatherhood is finally established, for the death of the Son is also in some sense the death of the father who is one with the Son.[23] This death of God Ricoeur sees in Hegelian terms as the "death of a separated transcendence". One is left, not without God, but without the separated God.

It remains to be seen whether this archaeology of symbols will bring any solace to the Christian feminist. Superficially the language of fatherhood is in place more firmly than ever for, in Ricoeur's scheme, it is this "achieved language of fatherhood", reached first by rejection of divine paternity in the Mosaic narrative, then by the designation of the prophets, and the address and invocation in the New Testament which finally colludes in its own destruction and opens the way for a non-patriarchal religion of hope.

Furthermore it superficially seems to blow a wide hole in simple versions of the "Jesus, the Good Feminist" argument where Jesus is styled as inheriting a religion with a dreaded "father God" and transforming it through a personal regard for women. This might be no bad thing, since Jewish colleagues rightly caution Christian feminists against achieving a "clean" Christianity by painting Judaism in dark colours. The real point, however, is that religions are not patriarchal simply in virtue of styling their deities "fathers" but rather by underwriting social patterns which privilege men over women. This could be the case in a religion which used no personal stylisations of God of any form.

But what real choices does the Christian feminist have? The least problematic, as I have said, is to reject Christianity altogether. If, on the other hand, one stays with Christianity one must come to terms with those sections of its texts and tradition where the symbolism is ineradicably masculine. Undoubtedly the new language of liturgy and devotion will be more inclusive and less masculine than that of the tradition. Some Christian communities may and maybe must elect not to use "father" as a divine title, given the pain it can cause. In the long run one is faced with Jesus himself, God incarnate in Christian orthodoxy, whose physical masculinity cannot be gainsaid. Of course, it is open to Christians now, as always since antiquity, to deny the divinity of Christ but this, while resolving some feminist difficulties, creates many others. Apart from the rupture with trinitarian orthodoxy, it is not clear one is any better off honouring Jesus as a male demi-God or supreme holy prophet. Indeed, I think this is worse. Better, again, to leave Christianity altogether.

The other possibility that we have only begun to explore is that while the paternal imagery remains in place in the historic literature at least, it be seen as a figure not "well-known" and "invariable" but, as Ricoeur suggests, as an incomplete figure that traverses a number of semantic levels. It is not a model there from eternity (the patriarchal father), but a mobile symbol whose sense develops through the Hebrew Bible, and which for Christians takes on a different sense in the books of the New Testament where "father" is known from the sister and brothers in Christ to whom God stands as *Abba* father.[24]

Jurgen Moltmann has argued that the name "Father" for God has two backgrounds, one in patriarchy, the "Universal Father" and "dreaded Lord God" (here the term is used metaphorically) and the other where God, literally, is father of the "first-born" Son.[25] It is the second sense which must be decisive for Christianity. "The patriarchal ordering of the world – God the Father, Holy Father, father of the country, father of the family – is a monotheistic ordering, not a trinitarian one."[26] The father of Jesus, on the other hand, both *begets* and *gives birth* to his Son and through him to the *twice born* family of God. Moltmann says:

> A father who both *begets* and *gives birth* to his son is no mere male father. He is a motherly father. He can no longer be defined as single-sexed and male, but becomes bisexual or transsexual. He is the *motherly Father* of his *only-born Son*, and at the same time the *fatherly Father* of his *only-begotten Son*. It was at this very point that the orthodox dogmatic tradition made its most daring affirmations. According to the Council of Toledo of 675 "we must believe that the Son was not made out of nothing, nor out of some substance or other, but from the womb of the Father (*de utero Patris*) that is that he was begotten or born (*genitus vel natus*) from the father's own being." Whatever this declaration may be supposed to be saying about the gynaecology of the Father, these bisexual affirmations imply a radical denial of patriarchal monotheism.[27]

While feminists may be dissatisfied with Moltmann's strategy of ascribing to the "father" the motherly attributes, this passage makes the ambiguity of the classical symbol obvious.

We can move things in a more radically orthodox direction by drawing on an unexpected source – Julia Kristeva's book, *In the Beginning Was Love*. A Lacanian analyst (of a sort) and French feminist (of a sort), Kristeva begins her discussion with Freud's observation that the foundation of his cure is "Our God Logos".

She continues to describe her own perception of the psychoanalytic task as one of making word and flesh meet, making the word become flesh in a discourse of love directed to an "impossible other". She develops her comments with an analysis of the Apostles' Creed, noting that in the Genesis narratives God creates by making separation. Separation is the mark of God's presence; the separation of light and dark, heavens and earth, sea and dry land, male from female. And this dividing and separating reaches a climax in the Christian story with the crucifixion, the desertion of Christ on the cross and the cry of dereliction. (To add my own theological gloss, this is the separation of God from God.) Yet it is because one is deserted, Kristeva suggests, that one may achieve ecstasy in completion and reunion with the father who, she adds, is "himself a substitution for the mother".[28] If her reading is correct the symbolic weight of this Christian narrative re-establishes a fusion with the Other who is both maternal and paternal. "So God created man in his own image, in the image of God he created him, male and female he created them" (Genesis 1:27). It is difficult quite what to make of this psychoanalytic approach but we might at least in future hesitate before stating too didactically which religious symbols are male symbols and which are female.

It is easier, if only slightly, to chart the history of symbols than to predict their future. Does the "father God" have a future? If Christianity has a future then the answer is probably "yes". But it would be reasonable for a dispassionate student of religions to wonder whether Christianity will survive the rapid changes taking place, around the world and not just in the privileged West, to women's self-understanding. In my opinion, Christianity now faces a serious challenge, and one that addresses core metaphors, narratives and ideologies (with Ricoeur, I find these three are closely related). It may be that Christianity will not meet the challenge, or linger on as a pleasing anachronism distant from the life of the cultures it inhabits. You may well think we are watching yet another stage in the death throes of a dinosaur. On the other hand, like Ricoeur I find the heart of religion in hope. The Christian religion with its complex metaphorical structures has shown before its remarkable resilience

and capacity to make vital response to new circumstances. It
will be interesting to watch how it does so now.

The Doctrine of the Trinity: A Way Forward for Feminists?

JANE WILLIAMS

In *The Quest of the Historical Jesus*, Schweitzer demonstrated that each age makes the historical Jesus in its own image. Over and over again, successive generations search the New Testament and come up with the Jesus most needed by their own age. Similarly, I suspect, our age makes the doctrine of the Trinity exemplify the kind of relations, and the kind of society, that we most admire. In what follows, I think it will be clear that I have a certain ideal society in mind, and that shapes my understanding of the Trinity – though it is also shaped by it. The belief that the creative source of life is not a monad but a Trinity, not a monologue but a conversation, gives a particular dynamic to the quest for "society". I do not think we should be too apologetic about making Jesus – or the Trinity – into idealisations for our own age. We are not free, of course, to *invent* them, but provided we keep a certain critical edge in this task, allowing the past and the future to judge our ideals, and provided we are always aware that God is not limited by the failure of our imagination, then I think it is quite proper for each age to do its own "translation".

In the Incarnation (that "scandal of particularity") God is committed to history as a vehicle for revelation – that means the particular history of God in Christ. It means too that seminal history mediated to us by the past generations of believers; but it *also* means history as appropriated by us. God's involvement in the particular is not limited to the past. What I am hoping to do in this paper is an unashamed bit of appropriation. No previous generation would have used these particular emphases, though I like to think that they would have recognized the enterprise in which we are engaged: the enterprise of making sense of ourselves and our needs in relation to God. As I have had to work at the doctrine of the Trinity over several years, for some of those years in the company of men and women of other Christian denominations, under the auspices of the British Council of Churches, it has been a source of dawning pleasure and amusement to me that I have increasingly found this most abstruse and abstract of Christian doctrines to be the one that over and over again illuminates my own theological concerns.

Let me say, first of all, that there are all kinds of ways in which the doctrine of the Trinity can be understood that are not at all helpful to feminists (or, indeed, to Christianity as a whole). On the one hand there is the kind of crude reading of the Trinity as three men, or two men and a bird (the feathered variety). So, for example, outside a well-known evangelical church in the centre of Oxford a year or so ago, there was a large poster advertising a lecture "The Holy Spirit: he or it?" It seemed to me then and it seems so now, that that is a silly question, and that there is, in any case, another possibility. The same kind of thing is going on, in a much more subtle way in David Brown's book on the Trinity. Brown has "a predilection for describing in detail the inner life of the Godhead",[1] which suggests, as one reviewer pointed out, the male camaraderie of the Oxbridge Common Room. There are few things more daunting to women, or more exclusive of them.

Another approach to the Trinity that I would wish to rule out, although it has sometimes been used by feminists to good effect, is the suggestion that we speak of the Holy Spirit as female. The disadvantages seem to me far to outweigh the advantages. On the one hand, it is based on rather dubious linguistic scholarship, of the kind that says "*Rauch*/Spirit is a feminine noun in Hebrew, and so the Hebrews obviously thought of it as a feminine entity". Do the French really think of a chair as a feminine object, just because it is a feminine noun? This kind of linguistic naivety seems to me typical of English, a language with no genders for impersonal objects.

Secondly, I reject the feminization of the Holy Spirit because the Spirit is, in any case, the least imaginatively accessible, the most shadowy part of the Trinity. If the churches were to start calling the Spirit "she" tomorrow, I think it would make very little difference to our life and worship. The exception might be the charismatic churches, though I think the "power" of the Spirit has an ambivalent role here already: on the one hand the "charisms" cannot be denied, and may be given to women as well as men, but on the other hand, charismatic churches often develop extremely authoritarian structures of command which keep women firmly in their traditional places. In all churches the Holy Spirit is seen as indistinct but mysteriously and unpredictably powerful. I think this is a bad role model for women: we have been indistinct and mysterious for quite long enough already.

Thirdly, and perhaps most important, I reject the feminization of the Spirit as a way forward for feminist debate because it leaves unchallenged our deepest convictions that there *is* sexual distinction in God. It allows us to go on seeing the Father and Son as male. It allows us to forget that all theological language works with analogy and metaphor. It allows us to believe that because we are projecting a seeming "wholeness of humanity" into the Trinity that we are avoiding the dangers of anthropomorphism. It may be better than nothing, it may go part way towards admitting that a single sex *Church*, reflecting only one part (the masculine) of one portion (the male) of its worshippers is a mockery. The trouble is that if we work with a picture of a male Father, a male Son and a female Spirit, there is almost no incentive to look at the divided sexuality in all of us, or, on the other hand, to remember what the Christian tradition has always affirmed – that God is not a sexual being. Since we must use pronouns of God, I would suggest a catholic mixture applied to different persons of the Trinity, as occasion suggests. I would particularly recommend following the example of writers such as Julian of Norwich, who unhesitatingly calls *Jesus* our mother. Yet Jesus was undoubtedly a man. He is about the only real reason we have for using male language about God at all, and yet it is *Jesus* whom Julian calls "Mother" because it is he who performs "motherly" functions for us in Julian's analogy. Jesus feeds us with his own substance, his "milk", and it would be a pity to be so blinded by the historical fact of Jesus' maleness that we fail to see the real illumination provided by the image of Jesus as mother. This is a much more direct challenge to our understanding of gender in God than it is to see the Spirit as feminine and leave unchallenged the "maleness" of Father and Son.

Let me highlight some of the dangers of unthinking feminization of the Holy Spirit by quoting two recently published books. The first is *Life-Giving Spirit* by Alwyn Marriage. She writes:

> God, we believe, is the source of all our loving, is perfect love. But it is arguable that for such a relationship of love to flower, femininity must be included within the Trinity; otherwise we shall have to concede that homosexuality is at the heart of our image of God. If, in exploring the ground of our being, the creator of the world, and the pattern of what life is all about, we are limited to three male "persons" loving each other with no need for any female contribution, then we have got it all wrong about the union of male and female being the finest flowering of human love. For such a picture of cohabitation within an all-male community does not accord with our normal view of ideal love. In view of this, it is amusing to conjecture that many of those who would most resist any ascription of femininity to God would probably be the least tolerant of human homosexuality.[2].

This passage makes it immediately clear that you can start talking nonsense very quickly when you talk of the Trinity in sexual terms. Let me begin then by making a point so basic that it seems should not need to be said at all: *God the Trinity does not have a body.* This should immediately alert us to the fact that any talk of "sexual relations" within the Godhead is bound to be metaphorical. What can it possibly mean to accuse a bodiless entity of homosexuality? This is nonsense "number one".

Nonsense "number two" follows from it: once you have, falsely, accused God of homosexuality then you have, apparently, a reason why at least part of God should be female. The author coyly does not suggest why sexual relations between two men and a woman are more acceptable than those between three men. Unless we are supposed to see the Son as the child of the Father and the Spirit/Mother? And what of God's relationship with us human beings, if relationships *can* only be thought of in sexual terms, and if married sexual love is the "finest flowering" of love, as the author implies, should the Church not set up a fertility cult of some kind?

Life-Giving Spirit shows very clearly the dangers of introducing sexuality into God. Some of these extremes could perhaps be avoided by a more careful use of "feminine" and "masculine" rather than "male and female". Alwyn Marriage does pay lip-service to this distinction, but in practice she always confuses the archetype with the sexual being. This is found, at some level, in almost all discussions that distinguish between qualities labelled "feminine" and "masculine". So long as qualities like "vulnerability, tenderness, patience, faithfulness, compassion, sensitivity, intuitiveness and poetic sensibility"[3] are associated with the "feminine" and "woman", be she human, archetype, or Holy Spirit, then all that is operating is an unthinking sexual stereotyping. In Marriage's book it is never clear whether the Spirit is "female" or "feminine" – both, perhaps – but either way, the only real change it effects in the traditional picture of God is the occasional use of a feminine pronoun. The "male" persons of the Trinity remain "male" and the relationship betwen the sexes, humanly speaking, is unaffected.

In fact, to call the Spirit "she" can become yet another way of *reinforcing* sexual stereotypes. This is, indeed, what happens in what sets out to be a very radical book by Leonardo Boff. In *The Maternal Face of God* Boff makes the astonishing suggestion that, just as Jesus is the incarnation of the second person of the Trinity, so Mary is the incarnation of the Holy Spirit:

> Virgin Mary, Mother of God and of all men and women, realizes the feminine absolutely and eschatologically, inasmuch as the Holy Spirit has made her his temple, sanctuary, and tabernacle in so real and genuine a way that she is to be regarded as hypostatically united to the Third Person of the Blessed Trinity.[4]

But what does Boff think this means in practice? In a section called "Mary's historical traits" (not quite as short a section as you might have thought), Boff lists the following: Mary is the Virgin Bride, Mary is Poor, Mary is Mother, Mary has the Fulness of Faith (but note that this fulness is characterized by an uncomprehending acceptance and a trust "without grasping the profound implication"), and lastly, Mary is the Valiant Woman. Even this last is not as hopeful as it sounds for feminists, since it is understood entirely in terms of her motherhood and her passivity:

> Conceived without the original sin that traumatizes and alienates our existence, conceiving Jesus in a state of virginity that she maintained throughout her life, becoming the Mother of God, participating in virtue of this motherhood – silently and unassumingly – in the process of our salvation, and finally assumed body and soul into heaven at the end of this earthly life, Mary is a woman *par excellence*.[5]

So this God incarnate in a woman is nothing but the old-style mother, with a few added traits, like perpetual virginity, that even the best mothers usually have to manage without.

Even granting that these two books are at the extremes of writing about the Spirit as feminine, it must be clear that there are real dangers in this approach to changing our picture of God as male. It smacks of a kind of desperation to show that Christianity *does* have some positive evaluations of women. In fact, I think it shows just the opposite. While we are still so unclear about what "masculine" and "feminine" are, about what the roles of women and men are and how they relate, the back-door introduction of a woman into the male Trinitarian club does not actually help at all, if she is still only the one who does the washing up and has the babies and is never introduced to visitors. The feminization of the Holy Spirit is not *in itself* capable of revolutionizing our view of relations between the sexes, or, indeed our view of God. The Spirit does not rescue women and draw them into the forefront. On the contrary, by association with us ordinary women she inherits our invisibility and passivity, as though she had not already enough of her own.

But this is not to say that I reject the important recognition that sexuality is part of what affects our perception of God and our relation to God. Christianity has far too often assumed that sexuality and bodiliness are peripheral to our essential, praying beings. Yet, as Sarah Coakley points out:

> It is a not uncommon experience among those who give themselves seriously to the practice of prayer that sooner or later they have to face their own need of an integrated sexuality, and of an inward personal balance between activity and receptivity, initiative and response.[6]

I am inclined to think that this kind of exploration should go on, as Coakley seems to be suggesting, largely in prayer and in the language used about prayer, which is so often strikingly sexual. To call the Spirit female is to increase polarization between masculine and feminine, rather than to work towards the "integrated sexuality" Coakley speaks of.

But if the doctrine of the Trinity does not serve us by putting a woman in high places, as it were, then why am I suggesting that it presents a way forward for feminists?

First, I believe the doctrine of the Trinity provides a vital corrective to the overwhelmingly *male* picture of God that Christianity tends to provide, and that it does this, not by giving God a sex-change but by making clear the *status* of the language that describes God as male. The dominant picture in the Christian Gospel is that of the Incarnate Jesus and his Father. This central relationship has captured our liturgical life, our artistic life and our inner imaginative life to the virtual exclusion of all other images. If you look at popular religious writing like, for example, C. S. Lewis' Narnia stories, there is no Trinity at all. Aslan is the son of the emperor over the water, and that is the whole picture; and yet this is an allegory from one who is assumed to be a great defender of orthodoxy. His imagination obviously had no place for the Holy Spirit.

In the same way, if you look at the work of many modern theologians, you will find a similar failure of the imagination. Even such an avowedly Trinitarian writer as Jurgen Moltmann cannot really show us the Spirit alive with the kind of life he feels in the Father and Son. In *The Crucified God* Moltmann has a vivid chapter on the death of Jesus:

> What happened on the cross of Christ between Christ and the God whom he called his Father and proclaimed as "having come near" to abandoned men? According to Paul and Mark Jesus himself was abandoned by this very God, his Father, and died with a cry of godforsakenness . . . The Son suffers dying, the Father suffers the death of the Son, the grief of the Father here is just as important as the death of the Son. The Fatherlessness of the Son is matched by the Sonlessness of the Father, and if God has constituted himself as the Father of Jesus Christ, then he also suffers the death of his Fatherhood in the death of the Son.[7]

This is because the simple truth of the matter is that our usual liturgical formula, "Father, Son and Holy Spirit" is not really Trinitarian at all; it is binitarian with another bit tacked on because you know it should be there. Father and Son are relational words. When you have them together in a sentence they tell you something, at least about each other. Holy Spirit is not self-evidently related to or illuminated by being put in a sentence with Father and Son.

One of the many results of the imaginative stranglehold of the Father/Son imagery is that it allows us to believe that God is "really" male. While traditional theology has always denied this, stressing that God has no body and is beyond gender, nonetheless, this denial remains at a theoretical level when all our most telling images are of a Father and his Son. Some of those who oppose the ordination of women to the priesthood in the Church of England are now forging a novel and radical theology that does make it *necessary* to think of God as more or less male (or at least more male than female), though not all would go as far as the journalist William Oddie in denying that paternal imagery about God is metaphorical.[9]

So let us be clear that the primary sense of "Father" is biological; that is the one that needs no explanation or imaginative engagement. God is not Jesus' biological Father, nor is God our

biological father. That there are many more important connotations to the word "father" is undeniable, but they are none of
them universally applicable wherever the word "father" is used.
This is not to deny that God is rightly and truly called "the
Father of our Lord Jesus Christ", and "our Father" too, but it
is to suggest that we are not making a clear, unequivocal statement that conveys the exact same sense and truth to all its
hearers. It needs imaginative assent and constant translation and
it seldom receives them both. Instead, we allow the primary
male, biological sense of "Father" to dictate the meaning in ways
that are sometimes even counter to the context in which the
metaphor is being used.

This becomes clearer, I think, if we look at the debate there
has been over the past few years over the Virgin Birth of Jesus
(by which people generally mean the virginal conception of Jesus,
rather than the technical physical virginity of Mary during the
process of birth-giving). Traditionally, the notion that Jesus was
born without the participation of a human father served two
purposes: the first was to emphasise the reality of Jesus' *humanity*.
He was really born, as we all are. This aspect is often forgotten
nowadays since we are not inclined anyway to think of Jesus as
a superhuman being. Secondly, it serves to emphasise Jesus'
difference from us, and this is where the debate tends to centre
nowadays. People seem to feel that Jesus cannot really be divine
if he goes through the ordinary processes of birth. To a culture
that believed that the woman merely provided an incubator for
the growing child, this "normal" aspect of Jesus' beginnings
could be seen to be largely irrelevant. But *we* know that the sexes
play an equal part in the production of a child, and that a child
lives from its mother's life in the womb. So if Jesus has no father
it seems to us that he is neither human nor divine. He is a
hybrid. Yet this is not the conclusion drawn by popular debate.
Instead God is simply slotted into the role of human father,
unthinkingly betraying that when we speak of the "fatherhood
of God" we have confused the latter with biological fathering. I
believe that the whole debate displays a very deep-rooted belief
that the first person of the Trinity *plays a male role* in relation to
Mary. Otherwise, surely, those who wished to defend the divinity

of Jesus on the grounds of his birth would have to deny him human parentage altogether? Yet if you were to suggest that God the Father plays the swan to Mary's Leda, it would be clear that what is going on is entirely indefensible in traditional Christian terms. Clearly, thoughtless use of the language of divine "fatherhood" has real pitfalls.

I think it is precisely to that kind of awareness that Trinitarian formulae bring us. I have already indicated that, where the imagery of Father and Son predominates, there is simply no room for the Holy Spirit. And yet our tradition tells us that God is *Trinity* and this discipline forces us to see that the language of Father and Son *is* metaphorical. It therefore gives us the freedom to suggest that a metaphor has limits. It does not necessarily draw on all the aspects of its original picture. We know that God does not have a body, so to call God "Father" cannot be a metaphor that draws on biology.

The strict Trinitarian formulae are not precisely metaphorical: to say that there is one God in three hypostases is not an image drawn from life, though it is obviously not an exact description of a state of affairs either. It is language that conveys no picture, but defines the conditions that must be met in talking about God. It is, in that sense, what might be called a "grammatical" formulation. It is not more true than the language of Father and Son. It might even be said to be less true in that it does not, in its baldness, engage us religiously but rather warns us of the limits of the dramatic theologizing that we do with the pictures that the Father and Son readily conjure. If we always held the Trinity at the forefront of our theological discussion, we would be forced to notice that when we call God "Father", we are using the vocative, as Barth has said. The work is *relational*, not abstract naming.

Let me emphasize that when I say "metaphorical" I do not mean "dispensable". We have all kinds of reasons for retaining the terminology of Father and Son because it is given to us in Scripture and apparently used by Jesus. It often works as a profoundly creative metaphor, involving us in a relationship with God, as it has involved Christians for centuries before us. When we call God "Father" we admit our belonging. But if we are to believe in "God the Trinity" we must be aware that "Father" is not God's *name*, and that we have not described or catalogued God when we have said "Father and Son"; we have merely indicated an internal and an external relationship that will be variously imagined by whoever uses the description. The doctrine of the Trinity is not so easily assimilated and dramatized, and its very abstraction helps to remind us of the dangers of making God in our own image.

This is not to suggest that there are two mutually exclusive ways of talking about God, that either you talk in Trinitarian terms, or you talk of Father and Son and a vague third. On the contrary, I am suggesting that the doctrine of the Trinity points up the vital force of what is at issue when we call upon the Father and the Son. Trinitarian language and Father/Son language are not saying different things, but pointing to the same thing in different ways. What then, do our two chief ways of talking about God have in common?

What does it mean to believe that God is Trinity rather than monad? What does it mean to believe that God becomes human and calls God "Father"? Both ways of seeing God stress God's openness, the fact that God is self-giving, the fact that God is community. These emphases are the second major contribution that a renewed doctrine of the Trinity could make to feminist theology. I have argued that, on the one hand, the doctrine of the Trinity throws new light on the vexed question of the maleness of God. I now wish to suggest that at the heart of the Christian Trinitarian tradition is a vision of a *society*; a society that is based on mutuality, a society where personality is defined in relation rather than in achievement, a society, in short, that is based upon a vision of the "society" of the Trinity. It is this society which the Church strives to emulate, perhaps with limited success. But at least there is, inbuilt, a knowledge that our communities as presently constituted do not reflect God's Trinitarian nature, and that we therefore have a right to challenge the Church to change.

Feminists have always had a certain suspicion of hierarchy. It seems true that one of the few things all religions have in common is the reinforcement of hierarchy and that in these hierarchies women usually end up firmly at the bottom. It is also true that a certain amount of hierarchical discussion does creep into the Trinitarian studies, under the guise of the "source" of the God-head. However, what is really at issue here is not which person of the Trinity comes "first", but how you can talk about unity and diversity at the same time. Hence the tortuous descriptions of who proceeds from whom in the Trinity, since God is _one_, even in threeness.[10] What is clear is that no member of the Trinity is King, even though their relations may be carefully differentiated.

Christianity has, in theory, a powerful critique of the will to power and of the structuring of society on the basis of the possession of power. We believe that God gives godself into our hands in the person of the human Jesus. We celebrate Jesus' _death_ as the heart of God's saving action on our behalf. Jesus' authority comes not from his strength but from his willingness to be weak and to trust in God, whom he calls "Father". And the Father comes to us as the one whose love we know through the life and death and resurrection of someone like us, that is, Jesus. God the Father is content to be not GOD to us, but the Father of Jesus, enabling us to call God _Abba_ as Jesus did. The New Testament also suggests that the Holy Spirit is the one who gives us those qualities that do help to make human societies a little more like the perfect society of the Trinity, qualities like love, joy, patience, kindness, faithfulness and so on.[11]

So what is going on in _our_ perception of the Trinity is a kind of circular movement in which each finger points to the other persons. The Father glorifies the Son, the Son glorifies the Father and the Spirit. The Spirit makes real the Son to us, and the Son shows us the Father, and so on. But this great circle of self-abnegation has not always been a useful model of society for women. Somehow women have often got landed with the role of building up others, but have waited in vain for others to bring _them_ forward to play _their_ full role. But in the Trinity each plays its proper role and we, in turn, are called to Christian discipleship and not to "good order". The Trinity is precisely _not_ a family, with a mother, father and child in proper hierarchy. It is a radically different society. However well the Church has adapted itself to hierarchical structures, such as the family, the well-governed state with a monarch at the top, a Church with an archbishop or better still a pope at its head, Christianity is in essence a revolutionary society where God's call *must* be heard and *all* must grow into the likeness of God's Son.

I do not suggest that if we were to convert the Church to a truly Trinitarian theology that the feminist new age would dawn. I *do* believe that the vision of the Trinity presses heavily upon those structures in our society that prevent people from growing into the likeness of that great circle of God's self-giving love. This is a love that delights in itself and in what is not itself, that creates in freedom something that is not itself and then gives itself into the hands of that other to be loved or denied, cherished or killed, as we choose. I suggest that such a God presses also upon a thoughtless belief in the *right* to self-fulfilment, the *right* to control of our lives and our bodies. The Trinitarian society is not just a critical tool for "us" to use on "them", but also a critical tool for us to use upon ourselves.[12]

The Biblical Account of the First Woman: A Jewish Feminist Perspective[1]

ELIZABETH SARAH

Introduction

I want to begin by explaining my perspective and the way in which I make sense of my task in writing this paper.

I am a Jew. My identity as a Jew has at least two implications for my reading of the biblical account of the creation of humanity – of woman and man:

First, my *general framework* of interpretation is influenced by the approach of the early rabbis who lived between 1500 and 2000 years ago. The tale of the "Fall" and "original sin" is not my story. According to rabbinic tradition, the first woman and man transgressed God's prohibition and so discovered their limitations as human beings, subject to God. When they left the Garden of Eden, they became fully human in both the physical and the spiritual sense – not only mortal and vulnerable to pain and hardship, but morally responsible for their own actions and capable of "good" and "evil". I am saying this in order to distinguish between the mainstream perspectives of Judaism and Christianity on the story of Adam and Eve. However, I shall focus here on the account of the *creation* of the first woman and man, and not on the tale of their exploits in the Garden of Eden.

My identity as a Jew is also crucial to my *method* of reading the text. My analysis is based on an examination of the Hebrew and reflects an awareness of the different modes of traditional rabbinic exegesis: *peshat*, the search for the plain meaning; *remez*, sensitivity to hints, the sub-text; *derash*, explaining the gaps, the silences in the text; *sod*, exploring the hidden meaning – the particular provence of mystical interpretation. My analysis will draw on *peshat*, *remez* and *derash*.

I am a Jewish woman. As a Jewish woman, I am responding specifically to the *Jewish, male* interpretation of the biblical account of the creation of the first woman which sacrificed *peshat* – the search for the plain meaning – in favour of an explanation which served to legitimate the subordination of woman to man. According to the tradition, Adam, the first human being was a "man". After creating the first man, God made two attempts to create a wife for him. We read (*The Legends of the Jews* by Louis Ginzberg, Vol. 1, pp.65, 66):

> To banish his loneliness, Lilith was first given to Adam as wife. Like him she had been created out of the dust of the ground. But she remained with him only a short time, because she insisted upon enjoying full equality with her husband. She derived her rights from their identical origin. With the help of the Ineffable Name, which she pronounced, Lilith flew away from Adam, and vanished in the air . . . The woman destined to become the true companion of man was taken from Adam's body . . .

Rabbinic interpretation of the creation of humanity does not do justice to the text we find in Genesis chapters one and two. The tale of the creation of woman out of man as an antidote to the uppity Lilith is not my story. I shall adopt the method, if not the content, of traditional exegesis, and begin at the beginning again.

I am a feminist. This dimension of my identity also has an important part to play in my approach to the task of reading the biblical text. I began to identify as a radical feminist in 1977. From this perspective, all "human" cultures and social structures are patriarchal: Men have invented Women – and themselves as well. From this perspective, the text of the Hebrew Bible was written by men and it reflects their experience and understanding in different historical moments.

I am a Jewish feminist. This self-appellation more or less sums me up – and everything I have said so far. My analysis is not a simple feminist critique of a male-authored text. The Hebrew Bible is infused with a consciousness which is not simply "patriarchal" – it is a specifically Hebraic consciousness, which includes both patriarchal and *holistic* elements – which run counter to patriarchal assumptions. Let me explain what I mean by this.

Within the patriarchal view of creation which we may identify in the Hebrew Bible, God, Creator-Father-Lord, creates humanity in His omnipotent image: Creation takes the form of a hierarchical order – humanity and animals over plants, humanity over plants and animals, and men over women – this last stage being outlined only following the failure of the first human beings to obey God – the ultimate ruler. Within the holistic presentation of creation, by contrast (which we may also identify in the Hebrew Bible) God, Creator-Artist, forms humanity out of the dust of the ground for the purpose of tending the earth. Indeed, God forms all life – human, plant, animal – from the earth – creation is One, as God is One.

These patriarchal and holistic conceptions are pure types. We do not find them as pure types in the two biblical accounts of creation, although as we shall see the first account is purer than the second.

The first account of the creation of humanity

In the first account of the creation of humanity, adam, the first human being created by God on the sixth day, is the pinnacle of creation. The framework is one of hierarchy and dominance, in which the "male" and "female" dimensions of adam play an equal part in ruling over all the animals. The purpose of the other living creatures is not mentioned – but the vegetation is to be the food for both adam and the animals. We read (Genesis 1:26–30):

> And God said, "Let us make **adam**[2] in our image, according to our likeness; and let **them** have dominion over the fish of the sea and over the fowl of the air, and over the cattle, and over all the earth, and over every creeping thing that creeps over the earth."/ And God created the **adam**[3] in His image, in the image of God, He created **him, male and female**, He created **them**./ And God blessed **them**; and God said to **them**: "Be fruitful, and multiply, and replenish the earth, and subdue it; and have dominion over the fish of the sea, and over the fowl of the air, and over every living thing that creeps upon the earth."/ And God said: "Behold, I have given you every herb-yielding seed, which is on the face of the earth, and every tree, in which is the fruit of a tree-yielding seed – to you it shall be for food;/ And to every beast of the earth, and to every fowl of the air, and to all that creep on the earth, in which there is a **living being**, [I have given] every green herb for food." And it was so.

God is first plural: "Let us make *adam*" (v.26), then singular: "And God created" (v.27)[4]; adam is first singular, then plural. The singular form of both God and *adam* is masculine, but the text is not describing the creation of a "man". Hebrew lacks a "neutral" gender; the male form is the norm. And so we read "He created him" and "male and female, He created them" – expressed in the masculine plural. In substance, the text is saying "He created **it**; male and female He created them". But just as the "image" of God in the account of the six days of creation is of an all-powerful, transcendent, Lord of Creation, so the image of the singular human being – made in the image of God – is of a master, ruling over the rest of God's creatures.

Adam is not a "man"; rather the first human being is made in the image of a man-like God. The differentiation of *adam* into "male" and "female" in no way modifies this image. The words *zachar* and *nekeivah*, which are translated as "male" and "female" (1:27) are symmetrical terms denoting anatomical differentiation for reproduction. *Nekeivah* is formed from the root NKB נקב , meaning to "pierce", and implies a being with a "hole" or "orifice". In this first account of the creation of *adam*, differentiation into two human beings makes the "multiplication" of humanity possible, which in turn serves *adam*'s primary purpose of dominion.

The second account of the creation of humanity

In the first account of the creation of humanity, adam is god-on-earth. God creates adam, which means that adam is not God, but it is not clear if there are any limits to adam's power. The text outlines adam's mastery, but does not say *how* God rules over adam. This is one of the problems which the second account of the Creation addresses. But the second creation story is not simply an answer to, or embellishment of, the first extremely condensed account. It provides an *alternative* perspective. First, the relationship of adam to the earth is totally different. We read (2:5–7):

> No shrub of the field was yet in the earth, and no herb of the field had yet sprung up; for the Eternal,[5] God, had not caused it to rain upon the earth, and there was no *adam* to till the *adamah* – ground;/ but a mist went up from the earth and watered the whole face of the ground./ Then the Eternal formed *adam* of the dust of the ground, and breathed into his nostrils the breath of life; and *adam* became a living being.

While the account of the six days of creation describes the multiplication of all the creatures as well as *adam*, vegetation is presented as an inert resource of food without a life of its own. By contrast, in the second version of the creation of humanity, an implicit connection is made between *adam* and the plant life which grows out of the earth: God forms *adam* out of the dust of the ground – *adamah* – for the purpose of ensuring the growth of the plants which cannot flourish without the work of *adam*. *Adam* is at one with *adamah* almost – differentiated from the ground solely in order to tend it. The almost is "the breath of life", *nishmat hayyim*, the breath of God: *Adam*, formed by God out of *adamah* becomes a "living being" with God's breath. And as a "living being", *nefesh hayyah*, *adam* is also at one with every other living being described in the initial "order" of creation – which upsets the hierarchical presentation of that order somewhat. Here we have a view of the world which is circular, not linear. In place of an omnipotent transcendent God creating an omnipotent transcendent "likeness" of himself, we discover an omnipresent, immanent God forming adam out of the ground and infusing adam with the "breath of life".

Adam is to work the ground, nurturing the green life which God has created. But still there is no word about the nature of the relationship between God and *adam*. This becomes clearer as we read on (2:8–10; 15–17):

> And the Eternal, God, planted a garden eastward, in Eden; and there He put the *adam* whom He had formed./ And out of the ground the Eternal, God, caused to grow every tree that is pleasant to the sight, and good for food; the tree of life also in the midst of the garden, and the tree of the knowledge of good and evil/ . . .
>
> And the Eternal, God, took the *adam* and put him into the garden of Eden to work it and to keep it./ And the Eternal, God, commanded the *adam*, saying: "Of every tree of the garden you may freely eat;/ but of the tree of knowledge of good and evil, you shall not eat from it; for on the day that you eat from it, you shall surely die."

God's first, positive, command, "be fruitful and multiply and replenish the earth", served to expand the powers of adam to god-like proportions. The second, negative, command has the opposite effect: The tree of knowledge of good and evil is off-limits, and transgression means certain death – or rather as we learn later, towards the end of chapter 3, mortality – returning to the dust (3:19). What is more, the garden itself – a specific area of the earth – places limits on adam's domain of action. The mighty *adam* has become a humble tiller of the soil, subject to the power of God.

But the account is not yet complete. Adam remains, *singular –*

and, so far, there has been no mention of the animals. Just as the purpose of *adam* as a worker of the ground becomes crucial to the growth of plant-life in the second version of creation, so the need of *adam* for companionship explains the formation of other living creatures – also "from the ground" – in the second version. We read (2:18–20):

> And the Eternal, God, said: "It is not good for the *adam* to be alone; I will make him a helper, corresponding to him."/ And out of the ground the Eternal, God, formed every beast of the field, and every fowl of the air; and brought [them] to the *adam* to see what he would call [them]; and whatever the *adam* would call every living being, that was to be its name./ And the *adam* gave names to all the cattle, and to the fowl of the air, and to every beast of the field, but for *adam* there was not found a helper for him.

Adam needs "a helper corresponding to him", *eizer kenegdo*, an awkward way of describing a being who is both a "support" and an equal – the word *neged* denotes the *eizer*, "helper" – a masculine singular noun – as an "opposite" in the spatial sense, a being apart, and on the same level. But in naming the animals, *adam* establishes their identities as living beings of another, unequal, kind and exerts power over them. And so *adam* cannot find an *eizer kenegdo* among the animals.

This brings us to the infamous misconstrued rib-to-woman story. We read (2:21–23):

> And the Eternal, God, caused a deep sleep to fall upon the *adam*, and he slept; and He took one of his sides, and closed up [the] flesh in place of it./ And the Eternal, God, built the side which he had taken from the *adam* into a woman; and He brought her to the *adam*./ And the *adam* said, "This is now bone of my bone, flesh of my flesh; she shall be called Woman because she was taken out of Man."

Throughout my translation, I have deliberately chosen not to translate *adam*, the word used to denote the first human being which God formed out of the dust of the ground, *adamah*. On the one hand, the word *adamah* is a feminine noun; on the other hand, *adam* is identified as "he" throughout. And on the third hand, it is clear in the account leading up to the splitting of *adam*, that *adam* is not to be understood as a "man". Indeed, the second account of *adam*, portrays the first singular human being with characteristics which patriarchal culture identifies both as **feminine** – for example, **nurturing** – and as **masculine** – for example, **naming**: *Adam* in relation to plant-life is presented in traditional feminine terms; *adam* in relation to the animal-world is presented in traditional masculine terms.

Unlike the first account of the creation of humanity in which differentiation into "male" and "female" is described simultaneously with the creation of *adam*, in the second account, differentiation is the outcome of a long process which begins by establishing the relationship of *adam* to other forms of life, and to God. It is only once the identity and purposes of the human species have been clarified that the differentiation of *adam* takes place. And it is against this background, that the account of the formation of woman and man should be understood. But the text is muddled. The Hebrew text abandons the logic of the account thus far half way through, and standard English translations, following the new logic of these verses, opt to change the meaning of *adam* right from the very beginning. According to the *peshat*, the plain reading, of Genesis 2:21–22a, the first new being which God separates from the singular form of *adam*, is a **woman**. My explanation – *derash* – of what follows, made in the light of this observation, draws on the hints – *remez* – in the text. Let us now examine the verses in more detail, and see how the transformation of *adam* into "man" takes place:

1) God takes one of the sides of adam while adam is in deep sleep (v.21). The root RDM רדם , conveys sleep which is extraordinary and full of foreboding – like the vision-filled sleep of Abraham in Genesis chapter 15, or the dead-sleep of Jonah in the bowels of his ship-of-flight. The word for "side", *tzeila*, a feminine noun, is used variously to denote – the "sides" of the Ark in Exodus chapters 25 (v.12) and 26 (vv.26–27), the sides or planks of cedar which panelled the Temple walls in 1 Kings 6 (vv. 15–16), and the "slope" of the hill in 2 Samuel 16 (v.13). So far, so good.

2) God builds the "side" which he has taken into a woman – *'ishah*, and brings her to the *adam* (v.22). What is the identity of the adam at this point? With one side removed, and the flesh closed up again, logic dictates that the remaining side needs to be "built" into a man–*'ish*. But this is not what the text says. The remaining side, is still the *adam*. The *adam* is undergoing a transformation of a different kind.

3) The *adam* identifies the new being as "bone of my bones and flesh of my flesh", and calls her "Woman (*'ishah*), because she was taken out of Man (*'ish*)" (v.23). But *'ishah* was not taken out of *'ish*. One of the sides of the *adam* was built into *'ishah*. The words *'ishah* and *'ish* are equivalent terms denoting a social relationship characterised by equality and interdependence.[6] Clearly, they are used here for the first time to describe the **outcome** of the differentiation of the *adam* – just as the words *zachar* and *nekeivah* are used in the first account of the creation of humanity to express the differentiation of the *adam* into two unlike "sexes" for reproduction. However, while the words *zachar* and *nekeivah* emphasise sexual **difference**, the words *'ishah* and *'ish* draw attention to the **similarity** between "woman" and "man" as social beings. Indeed, it is not clear from the use of the words *'ishah* and *'ish* alone, that these two forms of *adam* correspond to "female" and "male" respectively – although the word *'ishah* is a feminine noun. All we know from the **context** is that because "It is not good for the *adam* to be alone" (2:18), God has split *adam* in two. On the one hand, the two beings are two halves of one whole, on the other hand, they are two separate selves *keneged* – opposite – one another. The difference between them derives from the fact of **separation**, not from sexual difference.

If one follows the English translation, one might make the mistake of thinking that the problem in the text derives from the use of the word "rib". The Hebrew text tells a different story. The *adam* remains – minus one side – and in the same mould as the *adam* who named the animals. The logic of the account has faltered. The transformation of *adam* into *'ishah* and *'ish* is incomplete, and by staying in the picture *adam* has not only become identified with "man", but defined "woman" in relation to **himself**. And so we read (2:24–25):

Therefore shall a man leave his father and his mother, and shall cleave to **his woman**, and they shall be one flesh./ And they were both naked, **the *adam* and his woman**, and were not ashamed.

And so Woman became Man's "**other** half".

A conclusion

According to contemporary scientific understanding the basic form of human life is female – male anatomical difference is a modification of the female form. But of course man-made creation myths would have it the other way round. The second creation story we find in Genesis is an example of such a myth. But what is most interesting about it, is the extent to which it conveys a sense of the androgynous nature of the first human form. What we find is not a straightforward account of "woman" born of "man", but rather, a presentation which, while replete with linguistic ambiguities, reveals a logic of development from singular human being, into "woman" and "man" – two separate beings, different from one another because they are separate, but also alike, of the same kind.

How may we account for this? There is no doubt that the text is written by men. But it is written by men with other purposes than the explanation of the creation of human life in mind. Primarily, the first two chapters of Genesis are concerned with presenting the One God as the single Creator of the "heavens and the earth". On the one hand, this One God acts like an all-powerful "man"; on the other hand, this One God is both beyond images and descriptions, and encompasses all of them. And so the *adam* created by God in the image of God is both man-like and androgynous. Moreover, while differentiation of the singular *adam* gives rise to "male" and "female", two different forms of human being – for the purpose of reproduction; the division of *adam* into "woman" and "man", in order to satisfy the need for companionship, emphasises the essential unity of humanity. Indeed, it is only when the two creation stories are read in terms of one another, that "woman" and "man" may be identified with the two sexes, "female" and "male".

While putting the two creation stories together may provide a fuller picture, in my view it is more instructive to examine them separately, not only because they are different, but because I feel it is important to identify **how** they differ from one another. Having studied the content of the two accounts in some detail, I should like to suggest that while the first version is uncompromisingly patriarchal, the second reveals a concern for a holistic understanding of creation in which patriarchal elements intrude.

To summarize then: the first account of creation is **linear** and **hierarchical**, with *adam* at the apex of creation ruling over the animal world and consuming the plant resources without replenishing them. The differentiation of *adam* produces a dichotomy–"male and female" – although the implications of this dichotomy, the rule of "male" over "female", are not explored. Together, male and female exist in a dichotomous relationship with the rest of creation.

The second account of creation is centred on the *earth* from which all life comes and on the relationships between the different elements: The growth and replenishment of the vegetation is dependent on the work of *adam*; *adam* needs a partner, so one becomes two, but not a dichotomous pair. Creation is **One** – almost: *adam* acts like a "man" in relation to the animals, and in relation to the woman – undermining the essential **equivalence** of *'ishah* and *'ish*.

The Creation story remains incomplete – or does it? Despite the patriarchal form of the first version, and the holistic elements in the second, neither has succeeded in explaining the defining characteristics of the two separate human beings besides the anatomical differences suggestive of different roles in reproduction. Of course, the Book of Genesis goes on to provide this explanation in chapter three – which also becomes a **rationale** for the subordination of the first woman to the first man. From the point of view of the need to explain the unequal relationship between the two sexes, the creation stories we find in chapters 1 and 2 remain incomplete. But in an important sense the account

Women's Voices

of creation ends with the formation of woman and man – out òf *adam*. The patriarchal perspective in the accounts of the creation of humanity is modified by a holistic vision of unity. All the rest – the narrative concerning the woman and the "serpent", the eating of the tree of knowledge, the punishments inflicted by God – is commentary.

Feminism and Christian Ethics

LINDA WOODHEAD

Introduction: the feminist critique of Christian ethics

Ever since the emergence of feminism as a self-conscious movement, the feminist critique has been applied to Christianity. The
very rapid growth of feminist theology in the last few decades is
witness to this. On the whole, however, the feminist critique has
been concentrated on Christian theology rather than on Christian
ethics. Feminist theologians have given much attention to the
question of how to speak and think about God, Christ and the
Holy Spirit in ways that are not male-centred (androcentric)
rather less to that of how to speak and think about the sort of
people we should be and the sort of things we should do in ways
that are not androcentric, yet are grounded in the Christian
tradition.

On the few occasions that the attempt has been made to apply
the feminist critique to Christian ethics, the results have been a
little disappointing. Christian ethics has too often been presented
as irredeemably androcentric, a central pillar of patriarchy, the
only option for liberated women being to reject it or to reform it
radically. Christian ethics is said to advocate just that behaviour
which has the effect of oppressing women: the rejection of the

body, an unquestioning obedience to a male God, the exaltation of reason over feeling and of law over love.[1]

Yet this portrayal seems to depend upon a very particular – and inadequate – understanding of the feminist critique, an understanding which inevitably generates this negative picture of Christian ethics. According to this understanding the feminist critique is "an oppositional practice based on resistance to the dominant [male] hegemony".[2] In other words, the critique rests on the assumption that all men and all male thought and action are different from and opposed to all women and all female thought and action. So the feminist critique is a "hermeneutic of suspicion", one that exists to bring to light the hidden presuppositions of all male institutions and ideas, presuppositions which are inevitably misogynist and which must be repudiated. Andrea Dworkin presents this position at its starkest. She writes:

> The feminist project is to end male domination. In order to do this, we will have to destroy the structure of culture as we know it, its art, its churches, its laws . . . [3]

The assumption is that because all hitherto-existing human institutions – art, churches, laws etc. – have been created by men they *must* be hostile to women and must be opposed by women.

I do not believe that a feminist critique is necessarily oppositional. Many of the texts and institutions it is applied to will of course contain androcentric presuppositions, and when they do it is certainly the task of the feminist critique to bring them to light and to oppose them. But it is quite wrong to assume *a priori* that all male creations will be androcentric. It is wrong because there is no evidence that men and women are fundamentally different – that they have different *natures* – nor that they are inevitably opposed to one another. To believe that they are is to believe in just that sort of biological determinism – the idea that there is a fixed male nature and a fixed female nature – that most feminists say they want to reject.

In this discussion, therefore, I wish to apply to Christian ethics a feminist critique that is not *a priori* oppositional. I shall call it an "open" feminist critique. This critique does not assume a fixed and unbridgeable gulf between the interests and experiences of men and women, as if there were separate realms of reality to which access were granted only on the basis of sex. But it does make the more reasonable assumption that men and women will often have significantly different perspectives on things, due largely to cultural factors. As Virginia Woolf said of women:

> "We" – meaning by "we" a whole made up of body, brain and spirit, influenced by memory and tradition – must still differ in some respects from "you", whose body, brain and spirit have been so differently trained and are so differently influenced by memory and tradition. Though we see the same world, we see it through different eyes.[4]

In order to look at Christian ethics through women's eyes and in terms of women's interests, this open feminist critique will draw upon psychological studies of women and upon the writings of women, particularly of women ethicists. Because it will not assume *a priori* that Christian ethics is either sympathetic or hostile to these perspectives and interests, it may turn out to be a constructive rather than a destructive method. It may reveal meaning that is inclusive of women's experience, meaning that the massive male domination of Christian scholarship has obscured until now.[5]

Christian ethics: the twofold commandment

When the Pharisees heard that [Jesus] had silenced the Sadducees, they came together. And one of them, a lawyer, asked him a question, to test him. "Teacher, which is the greatest commandment in the law?" And he said to him, "You shall love the Lord your God with all your heart, and with all your soul, and with all your mind. This is the greatest and first commandment. And the second is like it, You shall love your neighbour as yourself. On these commandments depend all the law and the prophets."

(MATTHEW 22:34–40)

An initial problem facing anyone who wishes to talk about Christian ethics or "the Christian ethic" is to specify what it is they are talking about.[6] In the discussion that follows I will take as a summary of that ethic the above words of Jesus as reported in Matthew's gospel and paralleled in all the synoptics, for I believe they supply us with the best general statement of Christian obligation that can be framed. There is, of course, a great deal more to Christian ethics, but the 'more' is commentary on this passage.[7]

The discussion which follows is divided into two main sections, the first dealing with the form of the Christian ethic, the second with its content. This division is a loose one, and the terms 'form' and 'content' are not used in a technical sense: the former refers to the overall shape of the Christian ethic, the latter to some of its more particular characteristics.

The form of the Christian ethic

The morality that is summarised by the double commandment is a morality which focuses on personal relationship, relationship with God and neighbour. This distinguishes it starkly from other forms of ethic more common today.

Most importantly it distinguishes it from an influential contemporary conception of morality which sees the latter as concerned with the regulation of the competing claims of individuals rather than with the establishment of loving personal relationships.[8] Such regulation is to be achieved by the formulation of a hierarchy of moral laws or rights. These laws or rights must be regarded as universal: the same laws must be binding on all people, the same rights must be seen to be possessed by all people. If people obey these laws or respect these rights justice and fairness will be established. Justice not love is the goal of morality. For convenience I will call this the "justice and rights" conception of morality.

The fact that Christian ethics focuses on personal relationships rather than justice and rights may well be its most important point of contact with women's experience. For this conception of morality seems to be one that is much more acceptable to women, much truer to the way in which they try to live their lives, than any other. Women do, on the whole, seem to value personal relationships more than men. They are much more likely to define themselves in terms of their relationships than are men. And they are more likely to see the establishment of loving personal relationships as the most important goal in life than are men.

The most important way in which these generalisations about women can be tested is in the light of one's own experience: my own experience seems to bear them out, but readers will have to perform this experiment for themselves. Support of a more public kind is provided by some of the findings of experimental psychology. The work of psychologists like Carol Gilligan, who have investigated the ways in which men and women conceive of morality and make moral decisions, seems to bear out the greater importance for women than men of loving personal relationships.[9]

In one experiment recorded by Gilligan the following moral dilemma was presented to two intelligent and well-educated eleven-year-olds, Jake and Amy: A man called Heinz needs a drug to save the life of his dying wife. He cannot afford the drug. Should he steal it? Jake thinks that he should. This is his reasoning:

> For one thing, a human life is worth more than money, and if the druggist makes only $1,000, he is still going to live, but if Heinz doesn't steal the drug, his wife is going to die.[10]

Jake, in other words, constructs the dilemma as a conflict between the values of life and property, between the rules "You shall not steal" and "You shall not kill', between the wife's right to life and health and the chemist's right to protection of his property. He believes there is a hierarchy of values according to which life is more valuable than property, therefore Heinz should steal the drug. Fascinated by the power of logic, this little boy locates truth in mathematical calculation, which, he says, is "the only thing that is totally logical". Considering the moral dilemma to be, "sort of like a math problem with humans", he sets it up as an equation and proceeds to work out the solution, a solution on which all rational people would, he feels, have to agree.

Amy, however, approaches the problem very differently. Asked if Heinz should steal the drug, she replies:

> Well, I don't think so. I think there might be other ways besides stealing it, like if he could borrow the money or make a loan or something, but he really shouldn't steal the drug – but his wife shouldn't die either.[11]

When Amy is asked why Heinz should not steal the drug she gives an answer that focuses on the relationship between Heinz and his wife:

> If he stole the drug, he might save his wife then, but if he did, he might have to go to jail, and then his wife might get sicker again, and he couldn't get more of the drug, and it might not be good. So, they should really just talk it out and find some other way to make the money.[12]

As Gilligan comments, Amy sees the dilemma, "not as a math problem with humans but as a narrative of relationships that extends over time". She therefore, "envisions the wife's continuing need for her husband and the husband's continuing concern for his wife and seeks to respond to the druggist's need in a way that would sustain rather than sever connection". Amy also considers the value of the wife's survival in the context of relationships, saying that, "if she died, it hurts a lot of people and it hurts her". Amy's world is a world in which people are connected with one another, not a world in which rules are necessary to control the conflicting claims of individuals who stand alone. Problems only arise because people will not acknowledge this connectedness. So Amy feels that, "if Heinz and the druggist had talked it out long enough, they could reach something besides stealing". This would be her perfect solution to the dilemma: no relationships would have been disrupted, in fact a new one – the druggist's relationship of care for the wife – would have been established.

Further evidence to support the belief that women tend to favour a morality which locates the good in loving personal relationships and that they feel less comfortable with a justice and rights conception of morality can be supplied by considering the work of women ethical thinkers and the form of ethic which they defend. Do grown-up Amys still develop ethics which locate value in loving personal relationships? My reading suggests they do: in their theoretical explorations women ethicists tend to develop and support relational-type ethics and to be hostile to justice and rights-type ethics. Let me take just two examples: the French philosopher Simone Weil and the British moral philosopher Helen Oppenheimer.

One of the most central features of Weil's ethical position is her explicit opposition to the notion of rights, an opposition which she spells out in the opening pages of her last book, *The Need for Roots*. She considers the notion of rights an impotent and baseless one, dependent on the prior notion of obligations. The possession of a right is worthless unless someone recognises an obligation towards the possessor. As Weil writes:

> The notion of obligations comes before that of rights, which is subordinate and relative to the former. A right is not effectual by itself, but only in relation to the obligation to which it corresponds, the effective exercise of a right springing not from the individual who possesses it, but from other men who consider themselves as being under a certain obligation towards him. Recognition of an obligation makes it effectual. An obligation which goes unrecognised by anybody loses none of the full force of its existence. A right which goes unrecognised by anybody is not worth very much.[13]

In other words, Weil's hostility to the notion of rights seems to rest on her belief that if a person has a sense of obligation towards some other, then that other has no need to insist on their rights, and the notion of rights becomes redundant. If the person has no sense of obligation then the appeal to rights is unlikely to be effective in any case – unless the rights are enforced by the state. But state backing only gives practical not moral force, and it is the latter which Weil is disputing.

Weil continues her attack on the notion of rights by claiming that what a sense of obligation or duty (she uses the words synonymously) responds to is not a person's rights but their *needs*. She believes that the primary human obligation, binding on all people, is respect for persons. But this respect is only effectively expressed if it is made concrete in a response to people's earthly needs. She believes that these needs remain fairly constant through time and space, and that the basic needs of the human body (food, warmth, shelter etc.) are fairly easily spelt out. The needs of the soul are harder to identify, but Weil attempts to do so in *The Need for Roots*. She believes that it is to such needs and not to rights that the moral sense must respond, and on which social reform must be based. Morality is not about the regulation of the competing demands of separate individuals but about the recognition of our mutual interdependence and responsibility for one another.

In many ways Oppenheimer's attitude to a justice and rights conception of morality is very similar to Weil's. She too is very critical of such a morality, though she prefers to level her criticisms at the notion of justice or fairness (she takes the two as synonymous in this context) rather than at rights. She believes that the highest, the truest morality – which for her means the Christian morality – is completely different from a justice and rights morality. It takes a completely different form. As she says:

> Christianity is not "fair" . . . Christ's demands exceed legality and ask more of us than can "reasonably" be expected . . . The teaching of Christ is that a man does not insist even on his rights, that he loves his enemies, that he turns the other cheek . . . [14]

Oppenheimer believes that such a morality is not just an unrealisable 'ideal' set before us to reveal our sinfulness, but that ordinary people can and do obey it. Her examples suggest that women in particular often respond – whether consciously or not – to the "unfair" demands of such a morality. As she says:

A mother does not ask, "How little need I spend on presents for my children?" "How much may I punish them for being naughty?" or "What is it my duty to give my husband to eat?" She may find it difficult to decide how much it would be best to spend or punish or provide, but this is not a problem of law, and as soon as it becomes one of law she is to that extent not behaving like a mother or a wife."[15]

Where Oppenheimer differs from Weil, however, is in her appreciation of the important place that the notions of justice, fairness, law and rights do have in human life. Weil, recognising that such notions are bound up with the functioning of states and that they are only necessary in order to coerce people who have no sense of human obligation into behaviour that is not antisocial, dismisses them. Oppenheimer, however, recognising exactly the same things about these notions, affirms their importance. For human beings are sinful and do need to be forcibly prevented from committing certain sorts of evil, and stable societies and the laws that protect them are important. The notions of justice and rights are important and good in their proper place – in relation to the state – but they must not be allowed to claim as their own the domain of morality as well. They are necessary to control human sinfulness rather than to identify and promote human good. As Oppenheimer says, "The idea of a law which is 'just' makes very little sense as a kind of diluted version of Christian love, but it makes very good sense as an answer to the problem of human hard-heartedness."[16]

Taken together then, the evidence provided by women writers in the field of ethics as well as by some significant psychological studies supports the belief that women tend to favour a morality like the Christian which places central value on loving personal relationships over a justice and rights conception of morality. The reasons for this remain somewhat obscure, though some significant hints seem to have been dropped in the course of the above review of evidence. All suggest that it is cultural conditioning rather than any "innate tendencies" that is responsible: it is unlikely that women are born morally different from men, even though some sociobiological accounts would maintain this and some feminists would like to think so. Moreover, if innate tendencies were responsible it would be very hard to explain the fact that not all women do favour a relational type of ethic: interestingly it is just those women most influenced by feminism who tend to favour a justice and rights conception of morality.

The cultural conditioning responsible for the differences in moral thought between men and women is not too difficult to document.[17] It is quite clear that in our culture women are generally encouraged to care for others and to establish loving relationships and that they are valued for so doing whilst men are assessed more in terms of their achievement outside the realm of personal relations. Men may even be looked down on for taking personal relations too seriously: there is no feminine equivalent of the pejorative adjective "uxorious". This cultural conditioning probably has its origin in the traditional division of labour which ascribed to women the roles of carer/nurturer of children, husband, and elderly relatives. And as Oppenheimer has said, it is the establishment and maintenance of loving relationships which is required by this role, not arbitration on matters of justice and rights. The latter is much more likely to be a task required of those who work in the public realm – traditionally men – who have to deal with such matters as industrial relations, drafting and enforcement of legislation, distribution of resources, and so on. Even when this traditional division of labour begins to break down the conditioning may continue, passed down from parent to child even though its original rationale has disappeared.

The content of the Christian ethic

The above discussion has shown the central value which the Christian ethic places on loving personal relationships. It now remains to explore in more detail the nature of such relationships, according to the Christian ethical tradition as summarised in the double commandment, and in the light of the feminist critique.

1. *"You shall LOVE"*

What exactly is the Christian conception of love (*agape* in the New Testament, "charity" in the King James Bible)? Although it would be untrue to say that there is complete consensus among theologians on this issue,[18] a fairly solid agreement can be found among Christian commentators of all periods that at its most basic *agape* is self-giving equal regard for all people. It is only very recently that some voices have begun to challenge this agreement and to suggest that this view of *agape* may be in some respects inadequate and misleading. Interestingly, the majority of these voices seem to be women's. Often their interpretations of *agape* reveal features of the Christian conception of love which have been neglected or denied by male commentators. I will mention four such features which seem particularly important.

First, a stress on the *mutuality* of love. Many women writing about love feel that the hope and desire for a response of love from the one who is loved – indeed for communion with the loved one – is not only a natural but a legitimate aspect of love, and that there is nothing sub-Christian about it. They do not claim that love should be offered *for the sake of* a response, nor that love should not always involve a selfless desire for the well-being of the loved one. But they argue that at its best love is a reciprocal relationship rather than a one-way self-offering, and that it is quite right for Christians to acknowledge and desire this.

Women who write in this way are therefore critical of many of the traditional (male) accounts of Christian love which stress only the altruistic, one-way nature of love. Notable among such accounts is that put forward by Anders Nygren in his book *Agape and Eros*.[19] Nygren will not accept the legitimacy of any desire for mutuality in love and draws the sharpest of contrasts between *agape* and *eros*, defining the former as a one-way love poured out selflessly and with no thought of return, the latter as a love which is selfish because seeking some good from the loved one. The desire for a response of love typical of *eros* is what condemns

it in Nygren's eyes and relegates it to the realm of the sub-
Christian.

Helen Oppenheimer, one of the women ethicists who stresses
the ideal mutuality of love, attacks Nygren's understanding of
agape head on.[20] She does so by drawing attention to features of
the Christian conception of divine and human love which Nygren
neglects. Everywhere she looks she finds not Nygren's one-way
love, but two-way love. Our love for God is not one-way: we
love because he first loved us. God's love for us is not one-way:
God makes covenants with his people, he wants a response to
his love. And our love for one another is not one-way: it is often
a response to another's love and it in its turn hopes for a response.
Indeed human love falls short where one person is forever giving
love and the other taking, where there is no mutual minding and
mutual mattering, no give and take. As Oppenheimer says:

> "Give and take" is often recommended as a commonsense recipe for
> getting on reasonably well with our families or neighbours. It could
> mean more than that. A pattern of giving and taking, united and
> transfigured, is a good description of our best understanding of love.[21]

Oppenheimer believes that the best model for such "give and
take" is the Trinity, an eternal pattern of giving and responding,
an eternal mattering and minding.

A good example of the difference which a conception of love
as mutual makes in practice is provided by Amy's treatment of
the dilemma about Heinz and the druggist. The most obvious
altruistic course open to Heinz would have been to steal the
drug and to take the painful and humiliating consequences of
imprisonment upon himself. Yet Amy sees that this course would
endanger Heinz's loving relationship with his wife; it is important
that the two remain together, especially as she is ill. So Amy
suggests various courses of action that will not endanger the
communion of husband and wife, courses that depend on a view
of love as two-way rather than one-way.

A second important stress in women's writing on Christian
love is on *the legitimate happiness and fulfilment* which love brings.
This stress seems bound up with a view of love as mutual. For

it is the common experience of those who know true communion with another person that it brings great happiness. There is a good and unselfish reason why this should be: in mutual love giving happiness to the loved one brings happiness to the *giver*. What people want when they love one another is their own happiness and the happiness of the other as part of the same happiness. If it is a legitimate Christian aim to seek the happiness of the other, then it must also \be legitimate to accept with gratitude the happiness that others seek to bring me.

Just how common a stress on the moral significance of happiness is in women's writings is indicated by the fact that it is central to the work of two women as different as Mary Daly and Helen Oppenheimer. The "post-Christian" Daly places what she calls "lust for happiness" at the centre of her ethical scheme and even goes so far as to define feminism as "commitment to our [women's] past and future memories of Happiness in defiance of civilization".[22] She believes that such happiness is most properly sought in "interconnectedness" with others, in what she calls, "Be-Friending: the lust to share happiness".[23]

Oppenheimer is as determined as Daly to establish the legitimacy of the hope of happiness, though unlike Daly she tries to do so as a Christian. She cites the many affirmations contained in the Christian tradition that happiness is "man's (*sic*) true end", that faith is a recipe for such happiness, and that happiness consists in knowing and "enjoying" God. She argues that if God has made us to love – to love him and our neighbour – then it is strange to imagine that such love should do anything other than fulfil our true natures and bring happiness. And without ever minimising the reality and the power of suffering she maintains that, "The rising of Christ, for those who believe in it, is the pledge that the dereliction which is at the very heart of Christianity is not the last word."[24]

All this emphasis on the legitimate internal relationship between love and happiness stands, however, in marked contrast to the emphasis on suffering that tends to dominate many male accounts of Christian love. According to these, true Christian love is *always* suffering love. It is impossible to love properly if one does not suffer: there is an unbreakable internal relationship between suffering and love. And it is not only men who have maintained this: influenced by Christianity Simone Weil made the link between suffering and love so close that it is hard to tell where one ends and the other begins. In the attempt to become perfectly loving she implored God:

> That I may be unable to will any bodily movement, or even any attempt at a movement, like a total paralytic. That I may be incapable of receiving any sensation, like someone who is completely blind, deaf and deprived of all the senses. That I may be unable to make the slightest connection between thoughts . . . [25]

As Weil's words make clear, tying suffering and love too closely together results in the elevation of suffering into a goal of the Christian life. Many feminist writers have contended that the effect of this is to justify the suffering that women undergo in a patriarchal society. Suffering love has too often been a "virtue" imposed by men upon women, a "virtue" whose destructive consequences are only really known by the latter.[26] For if suffering and love are too closely identified then women have no moral option but to submit passively – indeed willingly – to the abuse, the beatings, the sexual assaults with which they are so often threatened. They have no right to expect happiness or self-fulfilment and must gladly accept the oppression they have always known.

Those women writers who deny the necessary connection between love and suffering do not, however, wish to deny that to love is to lay oneself open to the possibility of suffering: to love someone is to make oneself vulnerable to being hurt by them and by anything that hurts them. Ann Oakley shows clearly how love which seeks a response often brings suffering when she writes:

> The problem is feeling too much. Let me analyse it, because it is a female problem and therefore not mine alone: it is, moreover, a problem of love, of all the love stories that happen between men and women. In it is wrapped up the doggedness of dependence, the need for one human being to be affected by another. How can any of us

love without dependence, without laying ourselves open to the most horrendous conflicts and disasters?[27]

All that women writers want to deny is an *inevitable* and *God-given* connection between love and suffering. It is not at all clear that love grows out of suffering, nor that only the person who suffers truly loves. Love, if it follows its true course, should lead to happiness, not suffering. It is only when the course of love is obstructed (by sin and death) that suffering results. If the world were as God intended – if the Kingdom were fully realised – the bond between suffering and love would be broken, whereas that between happiness and love would remain.

A third important stress in women's accounts of love is that love is *a response to the unique worth of every individual*. Many male commentators have rejected this stress, emphasising the value of what is common to all people, not what is specific. In a famous passage, for example, Kierkegaard writes:

> Take a number of sheets of paper, write something different on each of them so they do not resemble each other, but then take again each individual sheet, do not be confused by the different inscriptions, hold it up to the light, and then you can see a common mark in them all. And so the neighbour is the common mark, but you see it only by the light of the eternal, when it shines through the differences.[28]

Other Christians express much the same sentiment by saying that people must be loved because God loves them, or because Christ died for them, or because they are made in God's image, or because in loving them one is loving Christ. What all these formulations do is to deny value to persons in themselves and to ascribe it to something outside them which graciously confers it upon them. The value of a person becomes something guaranteed by divine appointment. We love God through people; they become mere ciphers.

Many men seem wary of attributing unique worth to individuals because to do so seems to deny the reality of human fallenness. The doctrine of the Fall, however, is a way of insisting that all that is good in human beings comes from God – not that there is and can never be anything good in human beings. In addition, if human beings are completely worthless it makes it hard to see why God should bother to love us. As Oppenheimer says:

> If we concentrate entirely upon *agape* [in Nygren's sense] worshipping God only as the Redeemer who loves the unlovable, we risk neglecting God the Creator whose works were not made to be unlovable.[29]

And these works are created lovable in their concrete particularity. Each individual is of value because each individual is irreplaceable. A love which ignores this is worth little to its "object", and has nothing on which to get a purchase. It is insensitive and indifferent to those it loves and undiscriminating about them. It cannot accept that people want to be loved for their own sakes and for no ulterior motive, even if that motive is God.

Oppenheimer believes that such generalised love has little worth. She maintains that another sort of love lies at the heart of true Christian love, a love which responds to the unique worth of individuals and which she calls "appreciative love" and, more simply, "liking". She says of it:

> The love we are asking for . . . is something warmer, more partisan than acceptance. It is a kind of love that looks at what people see in themselves, that positively elicits their own special character and then is glad of it: a love that creates enjoyment and enjoys creation.[30]

This is the sort of love that friends have for one another, that mothers (or fathers) have for their children, that lovers have for one another, rather than the sort of dutiful obedience to God's inscrutable commands with which the word "charity" has now become identified in the English-speaking world.

In choosing to speak of Christian love in terms of "liking" rather than the cooler terms "regard" or "acceptance", Oppenheimer lays herself open to the objection that liking cannot be a central element of Christian love because it cannot be commanded and so cannot be a virtue. She disputes this, arguing that we can learn to like people and things and can do so by some sort of exercise of the will. As she says:

> There is a way of meeting the world with a readiness to be pleased, which is at least as much in our power as behaving as if we were pleased when we were not. Loving is not really any more within our own capacity than liking is.[31]

She refers to such an attitude as "attention", a word which is also used in exactly the same context by Simone Weil and Iris Murdoch.[32] To attend to the world is not to bestow value upon the world but to open oneself to a recognition of its value. I cannot will myself to love you, but I can give you more of my attention, listen to you, look out for what is valuable about you. Then I will almost certainly begin to like you. The seeds of love will have been sown. If the process comes to fruition my liking may even turn to delight in your presence, a longing to be with you and to know you better, to have communion with you. Liking may even turn into adoration or worship, attitudes which Oppenheimer believes are not only legitimate for human beings to have for one another (as the Prayer Book recognises, using the word "worship" in the marriage service) but the highest forms of human love.[33]

Oppenheimer's belief in the centrality to Christian love of liking points towards a fourth and final significant feature of many women's perspectives on love: *the rejection of traditional Christian hierarchies of loves*. These hierarchies generally put *agape* (gracious and disinterested love) at the top, *philia* (friendship) next, and *eros* (desire, particularly sexual desire) last. The hierarchies may take slightly different forms in the work of different authors, and different justifications may be given for the ordering they employ, but this basic grading has had great influence within the Christian tradition.

The grading reflects an ascetic bias in traditional Christian thinking about love. This asceticism is often inaccurately characterised as "rejection of the body", a rejection based on a gnostic opposition of the material and the spiritual. In fact such anti-materialism has always been condemned as heretical by orthodox

Christianity. Christian asceticism is far more concerned with the rejection of *desire* than rejection of the body, particularly desire for anything other than God. There are a whole cluster of reasons why desire is seen as dangerous. First, because it is not under voluntary control and so threatens the autonomy of the agent. Second, because to acknowledge desire is to acknowledge a lack and a need for something outside oneself. Third, because all things other than God are fragile and "corruptible". Even if they are not seen as unworthy of desire they are seen as transient and unreliable and likely to bring suffering to the person who becomes attached to them. Fourth, because to desire something seems greedy, too concerned with the self and its happiness. Given this suspicion of desire, it is not surprising that many Christians rejected those forms of love which involve desire – most notably sexual love – and elevated those which do not – most notably disinterested benevolence. Thus the hierarchy of loves developed.

All these remarks about asceticism and the hierarchy of loves can be illustrated by considering the writings of Augustine. Augustine is not an extreme example to take: he was a very moderate ascetic compared with contemporaries like Ambrose and Jerome, and unlike later writers like Lombard, Luther and Nygren, he was prepared to concede a limited legitimacy to human *eros* and *philia*. It was limited because he saw such loves as legitimate only when directed to God and answered by divine *agape*. Where they are directed to anything within the world, even people, they are sinful. God is the only thing humans should love as an end rather than a means, in the manner of *frui* (enjoyment) rather than *uti* (use). Augustine sees *eros*' incarnation in sexual desire as particularly sinful because he regards sexual desire as the most powerful of all desires and the one least amenable to rational control. The involuntary movement of the penis in sexual arousal was for Augustine the most powerful symbol of human concupiscence, of the fact that since the Fall men's bodies are no longer subject to their wills. Human friendship, though less dangerous than *eros* because more easily conquered, is still sub-Christian. It admits a need and develops a dependence. From the death of his friend Nebridius Augustine draws the moral that human friendship can only lead to suffering.[34] The heart should be given only to God. Human beings are to be loved only in a completely disinterested way, and not for themselves but for their orientation to the Creator.

Augustine therefore establishes a hierarchy of loves on the traditional model. The effect of his hierarchy was at best to marginalize women, at worst to victimize them. It marginalizes them because it gives so little worth to the love which women actually value and display. So maternal love, for example, does not even figure explicitly in the hierarchy, friendship-love is said to be unknown amongst women, and sexual love, the love women feel for their husbands or lovers, is condemned. And it victimizes women because it is a short step from seeing sexual desire as culpable to concluding that women, being the cause of such desire in men, must be responsible for sin and must be shunned.

When women consider the relative value of different forms of love it is striking how this anthropocentric ordering of loves is overturned. For few of the fears which men have of forms of love which involve desire for other human beings seem to be shared by the majority of such women. Women do not tend to cherish the rigidly individualistic ideal of autonomy that inspires many men, and refuse to identify holiness with being "set apart". Women are generally happy to admit that there is a "lack" in their lives and that they are not self-sufficient, seeing the attempt to deny this as an impossible and arrogant form of self-reliance. Women tend to acknowledge that to love someone is to lay oneself open to suffering, but believe that it would be cowardly to let that dissuade them from loving. And women do not on the whole believe that it is selfish to desire affection and communion, for love, though freely offered, should be two-way.

So in women's accounts of Christian love, it is the paternalistic, disinterested love (misleadingly called *agape*) which is relegated to the level of the sub-Christian. It is liking (*philia*) which is often valued as the first and most essential ingredient in Christian love. And it is the active desire for the well-being of another and for communion – including bodily/sexual communion – with them (*eros*) which is seen as the highest form of love which human beings can have for one another. In addition, women increasingly see the need to include maternal love within this scheme and to

claim it as a proper form of Christian love.[35] *Agape* is then
reclaimed to refer to all these forms of love when they are mani-
fested in a proper and Christian way, when they are "transformed into a mode of charity"/"made into the tuned and obedi-
ent instrument of Love Himself".[36]

2. *"You shall love YOUR NEIGHBOUR"*

The commandment to love one's neighbour is so familiar that it
is easy to overlook its significance. It is often taken to be the
equivalent of: "You shall love every human being as yourself".
But that is not what it says. It certainly does not say anything
less than that, but equally certainly it says more than that. What
is the "more", and how does it relate to the feminist critique?

In the first place a neighbour (in Latin, *proximus*) is a person
near to one. The command to love one's neighbour is a command
to love those near to one. The danger with this is that it may
seem to encourage some form of communalism: love for one's
own and indifference or even disdain for others. "Charity begins
at home" can have a horribly exclusive ring. Interpreted in this
way the command to love one's *neighbour* may seem to compro-
mise Jesus' ethic of universal love, and this is probably why it
is rarely taken seriously.

Any suspicion that the command to love one's neighbour
encourages communalism is laid to rest, however, by the parable
of the good Samaritan which Jesus tells in response to the question, "Who is my neighbour?". There are actually two neighbours in this parable: the man who falls among the thieves and
the Samaritan who helps him. It is the latter who Jesus has in
mind when he asks, "Which of these three, do you think, proved
a neighbour to the man who fell among the thieves?" In other
words, followers of Jesus are called to be neighbours to *anyone*
they come across, *anyone* they are "near" who needs their help.
It is the nearness and the need which create the obligation, not
any communal tie.

This account of neighbour-love is clearly one which validates
most women's perception that their chief obligation is to those

close to them, particularly to their own families. It supports their
sense that they have greater obligations to some people than to
others, something that moralists generally find it very hard to
account for. And it casts doubt on the worth of the universal
benevolence which some men mistakenly take for *agape*, and in
whose name they may give enormous time and energy to "chari-
table works" and neglect those closest to them. But this account
does not claim that neighbour-love must be confined to families.
Rather, it sees the love found within families (at their best) as
normative, as the *model* of the love that Christians are called
upon to show those outside as well as inside the circle of family
and close friends. The neighbour should be loved *as* family and
friends.

The basis of this stress on the moral significance of proximity
seems to be the recognition that we are embodied creatures,
limited in time and space, necessarily closer to some people than
others. It is perhaps an acknowledgment that people need to
share time and space and get to know one another in order that
the liking and communion so important to true *agape* can develop.

As well as encouraging us to take human proximity seriously
in our thought about love, the use of the word "neighbour"
encourages us to take mutuality seriously. For neighbourhood is
a reciprocal notion. As Augustine said, "nobody can be a neighbour except to a neighbour".[37] This is why there are two neighbours in the parable. So the neighbour that we must love must
also love us: the command to love one's neighbour insists that
love should be mutual, should be two-way. In this way the notion
of the neighbour reinforces the feminist stress on the mutuality
of love which I noted above.

3. *"You shall love your neighbour AS YOURSELF"*

In commenting on the twofold command to love God and neighbour, Kierkegaard described it as "a pick which wrenches open
the lock of self-love".[38] Kierkegaard was one of many, perhaps
most, male interpreters of Christian ethics who have seen that
ethic as primarily an ethic of self-denial and self-sacrifice. As

Daphne Hampson shows, they have identified pride as the central sin from which all others flow and with which all people are tainted, and have seen the Christian ethic as a crusade against it.[39] Yet the commandment to love one's neighbour "as yourself" suggests, as many women have noticed, that some form of self-love is assumed as legitimate within the Christian ethic, indeed that it can be taken as the starting point for love of neighbour.

Helen Oppenheimer explains cogently why it can be such a starting point. It can be – and should be – because nearly all people have a sense of being "a sort of living claim", of being someone who "matters" and who "minds" about things. To love someone else is to realise that they too matter and mind. It is to find out what they mind about and to come to mind about it myself. It is to see that they are a living claim in exactly the way that I am. To love is not to deny that I am a valuable and irreplaceable individual, it is to acknowledge that you are too.

Oppenheimer goes on to argue that self-denial is an impossible and an undesirable ideal. This is so partly because the conscious attempt to renounce self always has exactly the opposite effect: the renouncer becomes obsessed with his or her own self and its sinfulness. As she says:

> The conscious attempt to put self last could make us at best difficult to live with and at worst eaten up with spiritual pride. We cannot forget ourselves on purpose. What we need is something or better still someone to take our minds off ourselves.[40]

In addition, the person who really has ceased to believe in their own worth simply cannot love. They have no idea of what it is to value someone and would be unable to receive the reciprocal love which might be offered them and which has to be accepted in order for real love (which is mutual) to develop. The battered mother batters her own children. Moreover, self-denial makes a nonsense of the Christian teaching that *all* individuals are valuable and to be loved. To quote Oppenheimer again:

> Self-denial could never be an end in itself. "We were put into the world to do good to others. But what were the others put here for?"

If any creatures are to be loved and cherished, then sooner or later we ourselves are likewise to be loved and cherished . . . To shut our eyes to this for ever would be inverted pride or faithlessness rather than Christian humility.[41]

Oppenheimer's stress on the danger of self-denial is echoed in the writings of many other women. It is seen as a particularly dangerous ideal to be preached to women because they, already treated as worthless by a partriarchal society, may – unlike most men – actually take it seriously. Few men have depicted the horrific effects of renunciation of self as well as women like Jean Rhys, Simone Weil, Simone de Beauvoir, and Andrea Dworkin. In the passage below the latter describes the terrible paradox that women who really are self-less are in fact not admired for it, but despised. For to devalue one's own self is not to become saintly but to become needy and neurotic and less than human.

Inferiority puts rightful self-love beyond reach, a dream fragmented by insult into a perpetually recurring nightmare . . . The insult that hurt her – inferiority as an assault, ongoing since birth – is seen as a consequence, not a cause, of her so-called nature, an inferior nature . . . Her experience is recast into a psychologically pejorative judgment: she is never loved enough because she is needy, neurotic, the insufficiency of love she feels being in and of itself evidence of a deep-seated and natural dependency.[42]

Noting that women do often suffer from debilitating lack of self-love, as Dworkin so powerfully shows, and that an ethic which praises self-denial cannot but harm such women, many feminists have tried to turn the tables on male ethicists by commanding self-love. But I think that Dworkin's comments can also provide us with a clue as to why in the twofold commandment self-love, though acknowledged as proper and necessary by the words "you shall love your neighbour as yourself" is not directly commanded. The reason seems to be that self-love *cannot* be commanded. All that commanding someone to love themself can achieve is an inward-looking self-concern that is sometimes mistaken for self-love. The way one really comes to self-love is not by loving oneself, but by being loved by others – even "an" other. Women who suffer from lack of self-worth cannot be told to think better of themselves, they have to be shown that they are valuable by being loved. This brings us to the context and final part of the double commandment:

4. *"You shall love the Lord your God with all your heart and with all your soul and with all your mind"*

This discussion of feminism and Christian ethics has largely (and deliberately) confined itself to a consideration of love for persons and said little about love for God. Yet it would be untrue to Christian ethics to leave it at that. For the commandment to love one's neighbour only comes *after* the commandment to love God, and the latter is described as the greatest and first commandment, the one which demands all a person's heart, soul and mind. That being so, how can Christianity really claim to take seriously love for persons at all? The answer seems to be that loving persons is an essential *part* of loving God, and has a particular sort of priority. The First Letter of John explains this priority in the following terms: "If anyone says, 'I love God', but hates his brother, he is a liar; for he who does not love his brother whom he has seen, cannot love God whom he has not seen" (4:19,20). Love of God and love of persons are different things – hence the two commandments – yet love of God requires love of persons.

At this point it is necessary to face the objection with which the previous section ended: if the Christian ethic demands loving relationships with God and neighbour, and if the unloved person is unable to love, what of the many women who do feel themselves unloved? How can they be commanded to love? If the double commandment stood alone in Christianity, that would be a serious objection. But if it did, Christianity would be ethics, not gospel. Rather, the double commandment stands within the context of the promise of God's steadfast love for humanity, a promise made to Israel and fulfilled in the person and work of Christ. This promise offers a way out of the cycle of lovelessness.

It is the pick that wrenches open the real lock for many women, the lock of paralysing, inward-looking, dependence-inducing lack of self-confidence and self-worth. The assurance that we are loved frees us to love, it bestows a freedom which is far greater than "autonomy". Far from keeping women in subjection then, Christianity actually offers them "liberation"; the greatest liberation is reserved for those who have previously been the most despised.

Conclusion

My concern in this feminist critique of Christian ethics has been only to consider the basic nature of the Christian ethic, not to deal with its treatment of specific moral issues. There is still a great deal more work to be done in the latter area, and women have only recently begun to consider from their perspectives the adequacy of Christian teachings on particular moral issues. Their interest at the moment is largely confined to issues which bear directly on their sex, issues such as abortion, birth control, artificial birth techniques, and sexuality. Though I have not attempted to discuss particular moral issues, a non-sexist Christian ethic such as emerges from the feminist critique should provide a good basis for exploring them. To take just one issue – that of divorce – as an example: if Christianity is concerned with the establishment of loving personal relationships in which there is communion between partners, then the genuine failure to achieve such communion and establish a truly loving partnership may well be a good ground for allowing divorce (whereas if love is seen as self-sacrifice, it would not be). In such ways general remarks about a non-sexist Christian ethic may have very concrete applications.

Bringing the feminist critique and Christian ethics together seems to have shed some light on both. With regard to Christian ethics it has exposed some interpretations of this ethic which have the effect of taking men's interests more seriously than women's, but shown that in most cases these interpretations do not illuminate the Christian ethic as well as the alternative interpretations offered by women. This seems to indicate that the Christian ethic – and the Gospel insofar as this forms its context – is one that does not necessarily assume nor reinforce the inferiority of women. And with regard to the feminist critique itself, its application to Christian ethics seems to have demonstrated that it is not necessarily the anarchic and destructive tool it is sometimes supposed to be, but that it may liberate meaning that has previously been ignored. Christian ethics and feminism may after all turn out to be mutually illuminating rather than mutually destructive.

The Battle of the Sexes: or If You Can't Beat Them, Join Them

LYNNE BROUGHTON

One of the interesting features of human life is the ease with which we recognise each other's sex and the importance we attach to being able to do so. I can spend a considerable amount of time in conversation with a dog and yet be unaware which sex it is. I am always aware very quickly whether I am talking to a man or to a woman; even a brief glimpse in the street is usually enough for me to tell whether it is a man or a woman I have caught sight of, even in these days of "unisex" dressing. If I wish to ascertain the sex of a dog with whom I have become acquainted, the natural way would be to look at its genitals; yet I can recollect not a single occasion on which I have used this method to decide whether I am with a man or a woman. I have never done so, nor have I ever felt the need to do so. It is very rare indeed to be in any doubt of the sex of a particular human being. There are, of course, the cases of sex-change and transvestism which somewhat muddy the clarity of the distinction; but in fact, as we shall see, they only underline the evident importance to human life of a clear distinction between the sexes.

So it seems we have a distinction between what is constitutive of sexual difference and what is symptomatic.[1] Different genitals are constitutive; different clothing is symptomatic. What one generally goes by in the human case is things symptomatic rather than constitutive of sexual difference, and yet we have quite reliable knowledge of the sex of human beings. This is actually surprising, because symptoms are not usually so reliable, being only contingently connected with that of which they are symptoms. Consider credit-worthiness, and our need to judge whether an individual is financially well off. Even in our culture where we are very sensitive to all sorts of cues, clothing, accent, type of car etc., the symptoms are not very reliable. The well-spoken, expensively dressed person may be deeply in debt; the scruffy tramp-like figure may enjoy all the wealth of an internationally famed professor of philosophy. So it ought to provoke our interest that symptoms for sex are so reliable.

Of course, there are some few cases where the symptomatic is at odds with the constitutive. Men who have passed themselves off as women, or women as men, are not unknown. This can happen because the symptomatic is important and rarely questioned. If the symptoms are sufficiently thoroughly adopted few if any questions will be asked about the constitutive. When cases of cross-identity are found out it is usually because of the unexpected interference of constitutive features – to the recognition of physical attributes that are at odds with the symptomatic characteristics being displayed. To give just two examples: a) Recently the English gutter press has been delightedly covering the case of a sixteen-stone fishmonger who is said to have dressed up as an officer in the Women's Royal Army Corps, in which guise he/she seduced a number of supposedly unsuspecting young men from the nearby (male) army barracks. b) An adventurous young white woman, travelling alone through remote areas of New Guinea, was frequently taken by local tribesmen to be a man because they thought that a woman could not thus travel alone and unaided for large distances over difficult terrain. One tribe even initiated her as a man into the male secrets of the tribe.[2]

In the first of these examples there was deliberate intent to mislead, though we may well doubt how thoroughly the victims were in fact deceived. In the second example there was no intent to mislead, but the woman's behaviour was so at odds with expectations that members of the tribe were simply unable to see her as a woman. Evidently, if the cultural indications conflict with the biological, we tend to accept the former. (Perhaps one should add that she is not, to Western eyes, at all masculine looking.) These examples, and others like them, are interesting and newsworthy because they are rare, they cut across basic categories of experience.

What they highlight, because they are exceptional, is the strength of our cultural expectations concerning these symptomatic differences. We, that is all human social groups, take great care to make the symptomatic reliably symptomatic. The social world is one in which induction can work easily because we so design it. We have uniformity, but of culture rather than nature. The machines, artifacts and institutions created by human beings are largely predictable (save of course for occasional breakdowns) whereas there are few aspects of nature whose behaviour can confidently be predicted in advance. Natural processes may be reliable; and the predictability of culture is dependent on this reliability of nature. But dependable predictability is more obvious with cultural than with natural features.

The common trend of culture is to provide as much predictability as possible. This provides a background of confidence, freeing individuals to concentrate on other pursuits. Cultural pressures to make sexual differences predictable are among the very strongest. This shows itself in many ways. One instance has to do with my naming my she-cat "Fido". On being told of this many people reacted with a distress close to outrage. In most cases the distress was explained as a reaction, not to giving a dog's name to a cat but to giving a male name to a female. Crossing the sexual divide seems to be greater than crossing the divide between species. It is in such a context, I would suggest, that one must seek to understand the tendency of many sociobiologists to write as if the similarity between all male (or all female) mammals were greater than the similarity between all humans. They clearly perceive the sexual divide as greater than the divide between the species. But they see it as a natural given rather than as a culturally produced fact.

These remarks also provide a new perspective on the tendency in some circles to theorise about how the opposite sex is radically "other". Sometimes such talk is symmetrical, in that it takes men to be "other" to women as well as women being "other" to men. But very often the male view is taken as normative (I will write more on this below) so that then women become essentially "other". To the latter view belong the many pronouncements about the mysteriousness of women, their unpredictability, intuitiveness and inscrutability. A fine example of the former is a paper read by a certain moral theologian, arguing that heterosexuality is obviously better than homosexuality because in relating sexually to someone of the opposite sex one is relating to that which is "other" rather than to that which is essentially similar.[3]

Taking this argument to its logical conclusion would seem to imply that bestiality is even better than heterosexuality, since it involves a partner considerably more "other" than a human being of the opposite sex. But our moral theologian, and presumably many who use these concepts, does not wish to press the point so far. The idea of the "other" looks absolute, but is in fact to be confined to the human species. The similarities which men and women share by virtue of being human are not thought about; the discourse then continues as if there were no important similarities.

The differences between the sexes, within any given cultural group, are clear and reliable. Across cultures, especially between cultures that have not been influenced by each other, the differences may not be so clear. Our female explorer shows both that cultural pressures are strong (since she was firmly categorised as male) and that they are culturally relative, in that what they press you to do differs from culture to culture.

Although both men and women are subject to such cultural pressures, their extent and effect differs for each sex. Women who step out of line are subject to stronger pressure than men. Cultural pressures make women deviate more from the natural than they make men deviate from what is natural for men, and they leave women with fewer alternatives than men. It takes more to make a woman than it does to make a man; women need to undergo an elaborate process of feminization.

In Western societies this can be illustrated by the domain of cosmetic surgery. By far the bulk of such medical attention is directed at women. Ear-piercing and face-lifting are done mainly on women. Things like breast-restructuring and abortions are done entirely on women, for obvious reasons, but there seems to be no male counterpart. The example of sex-change operations looks like an exception, since most of such operations until recently have been done on men. But it is in fact, when you think about it, a form of feminization. It is another example of the belief that femininity is constructable, something to be worked at and achieved rather than provided by nature. Quite apart from non-curative surgery, remember that there are gynaecologists, but no comparable specialism for men, no andrologists. There is basic, normal medicine; then one can specialise in various peculiar things – a special disease, a special part of the body, a special sex.

The construction of femininity might also go some way to explaining why there is generally less outrage at masculine women than at feminine men. Women can dress in a wide range of styles, even in clothes made for men, without necessarily being considered strange. Indeed, sometimes such dressing enhances their femininity: consider Marlene Dietrich in her most famous roles. The prevalence in fiction from Shakespeare to Georgette Heyer of young women temporarily disguising themselves as boys may also be due to this enhancement. It is, on the other hand, very rare for men to be seen in women's clothes. When they do so dress it is usually for explicitly comic, even burlesque purposes and such is its only acceptable form. Otherwise even the slightest touch of femininity in male dress tends to be strongly condemned.

Further examples are not difficult to find. It was one of the charges levelled at Joan of Arc that she dressed as a man, such behaviour being considered immoral by the Church. But this has been no bar to her popularity and even her canonisation. There is no example of a male saint who is notorious for having dressed as a woman.

There is a similar asymmetry with names. Girls are frequently given masculine-sounding names. Lots of P. G. Wodehouse girls have nicknames like "Bobby", especially the girls who are not soppily over-feminine. It is a sign that they are energetic, that they might almost be male. The boys however never have girls' names. More generally, many girls' names are formed by altering boys' names. Thus Charles becomes Caroline, George Georgina, William Wilhelmina and so on. In Catholic countries boys are frequently given the name "Maria" or "Marie" in honour of the Virgin Mary but usually, as far as I have been able to ascertain, only as a middle name in conjunction with a masculine name.

So this naming is symbolic of religious devotion rather than functioning as a normal name. The implication of all this is that masculinity is normative whereas femininity can be constructed in various ways which contrast with the norm. It may be possible to construct a woman out of a man but never to construct a man out of a woman. A man cannot be constructed, he just is. This way of expressing it is admittedly far too bald and extreme but something like it seems to underlie much of the asymmetry about sexual differentiation.

One fact that bears this out is the difference between men who want to become women and women who want to become men.[4] Until very recently there were few of the latter. Lately there has been an increase in the number of women seeking sex-change surgery. There seem to be two reasons for this. First, it was generally considered that women do not face the same problems as do men. They can, after all, dress as men and they have a wider range of behaviour available to them so that their femaleness need not seem too constricting. Second, surgical techniques for changing males into females were developed much earlier than those for changing females into males. These are not actually incompatible with what I have been arguing. The latter reason is even part of my point. Because everyone is interested in putting energy into constructing women it is not surprising that these techniques were developed first.

The suggestion that women have fewer problems about their femaleness connects with what seems *prima facie* to be an objection to what I have been saying. This is the claim that, rather than femininity being something that is achieved only by much effort, it is in fact more difficult to be a man than to be a woman. This was illustrated very neatly some years ago in a television documentary entitled "The Fight to be Male". The film was not, as one might be forgiven for assuming, about initiation rites or war, but about the development of the human foetus from conception to birth. True to the import of the title, this development was throughout described in terms of the male foetus' fight to differentiate itself, to escape from the possibility of being female. As far as I was able to ascertain, this way of explaining foetal growth aroused no significant protest or complaint. It seems to have been accepted as a normal and accurate "factual" account. A number of biologists with whom I have had discussions have found it very difficult indeed to understand why there should be any objection to such a characterisation.

On a more scholarly level are some psychoanalytic accounts which highlight the different growth experiences of males and females between birth and adolescence. These emphasise, along more or less Freudian lines, the crucial part played by the mother in the child's early development. Mother is much closer to the child than father; the baby identifies with mother rather than father. As it grows older and must discover its own sexual identity it must differentiate itself from mother. For girls this is an easy matter since differentiation need only be partial; mother is of the correct sex to identify with. Boys must make a much greater break and turn right away from mother to identify themselves with father, a much more difficult and painful task.[5]

On this view, as with the biological example, the female is the default setting: unless some definite interference takes place any foetus or child will by a kind of inertia turn out female. To be a male is difficult, femininity is a constant trap, so one must be very careful about boys doing feminine things. It is the unsettled character of male sexuality ("the gentleman doth protest too much") which leads men to think of themselves as natural, the female as a cultural construct. What is more, men have no biological way of demonstrating their fertility once and for all as women have through bearing children; and this is absolutely constitutive of one's masculinity. Not even begetting children does this for men, since (without stringent precautions) there can always be some doubt as to a child's paternity (which may be why such stringent precautions are so often taken).

A small amount of reflection will make it clear that this line of argument is perfectly compatible with what I have been saying earlier in this paper. It takes more to make a woman in terms of superficial feminine characteristics. In particular women are subjected to greater pressures than men to conform to a visual ideal of attractiveness. It takes more to make a man on the deeper level of sexual orientation and emotional stability, though men face fewer pressures to bring their looks into line with a particular ideal, barring any lapses into effeminacy. Shaving might seem to be an objection to this, since it brings the male somewhat closer to a feminine visual ideal, but it does not run seriously counter to my views. In societies where it is fashionable or normal for men to be clean shaven this state is not perceived as at all feminine but rather as expressing a particular form of masculinity, such as for instance the way in which the Romans considered a beard to be the mark of a barbarian.

Both sexes are subjected to cultural pressure to behave consistently as either a man or a woman. It is time to give some thought to the nature and value of that pressure. At first sight it might seem as though being subjected to cultural pressure must be a bad thing. Strongly prevailing patterns of political and educational argument in the 1960s and 1970s throughout the Western democratic countries suggested that any pressure for an individual to conform to others' expectations constituted an unwarranted interference with that person's freedom. The results of this, especially in the field of education, have been well nigh disastrous. Taken to its logical conclusion, it would imply that parents should not teach their children a particular language since this would inhibit their creativity by confining their thoughts within the limits of one (or a small number of) natural language(s). This is of course ludicrous: a child who grows up knowing no language would have indefinitely fewer options available to it than would a child who learns only one language.

A language may in some ways constrain our thinking, but some such constraints are necessary to allow us the very wide possibilities of thought that we can have only because we possess language. Study of other animals has shown clearly that adult sexual behaviour is linked to what the infant learns. Even with birds, whose sexual responses are quite strongly controlled by instinct, it is necessary that they grow up with members of their own species in order to show the appropriate sexual responses as adults. By a process known as imprinting young birds (and the young of some other species) become attached to the animal that cares for them. At sexual maturity they will respond to the kind of animal with which they have become imprinted. Since they are usually cared for by members of their own species this does not cause great problems. But should they for example be brought up entirely in human company they become incapable of sexual response to their own species.

With primates it has also been shown that a young animal brought up without the normal company of a mother and other members of the species will grow up sexually inept. The correct pattern of sexual responses seems to be acquired or learned during the early years and cannot easily be learned once sexual maturity has been reached. There is psychological evidence concerning humans also which would seem to indicate that certain kinds of deprivation in infancy and childhood lead to uncertainty of sexual orientation in adulthood. Such evidence shows that interference in the circumstances within which the young grow up can have serious consequences. What is standard among members of a species is not likely to be interfered with; for example, the vast majority of infants of most species are brought up under conditions that are normal for that species. So likewise bringing up human children in circumstances where they could not be aware of clearly differentiated sexes would probably not do any good, given that this is the characteristic way that children are brought up. There seems to be some reason to believe that clear and unambiguous differences between the sexes are necessary for children to learn and for adults to engage successfully in sexual activity.

Is it necessary for culture to build on and accentuate biological differences? The universal prevalence of cultural pressures toward a clear differentiation of the sexes would seem to suggest that it is. All cultures require that there be two, and only two, sexes although some provide marginal roles for a small number of individuals who cannot conform. It is well known that some human babies are born with genital features that do not clearly determine them as male or female. Some are true hermaphrodites, possessing the genital organs of both sexes; others possess genital organs that are partly male and partly female. It might be thought that such individuals must grow up with a similarly indeterminate idea of their sexual identity, but not so. The crucial factor seems to be upbringing. If (as usually happens) the midwife or obstetrician confidently assigns a sex to the baby and the parents treat it as a member of that sex it will grow up with a clear sexual identity, experiencing no more problems than is normal with human beings. And this seems to be so even in cases where the structure of the genitals is grossly at variance with the assigned sex. Modern surgical procedures make it possible, now, to tidy up the genitals of such unfortunate infants at an early stage to bring the body into line with cultural expectations.

On the other hand it seems, contrary to popular belief, that most of those individuals who are seeking sex-change surgery do not suffer from such physical indeterminacy. The problem, as they perceive it, is that their (normal, unambiguous) genitalia and corresponding assigned sex do not correspond with the way they feel they really are. "I am a woman in a man's body" is a classic description of their predicament. So despite the fact that they are seeking a physical solution to their problem, the problem itself lies not only with their bodies but also with the identity which they have been assigned. Much discussion about the relations between the sexes has proceeded as if what is due to biology or "nature" is fixed and unchangeable, whereas what is due to "nurture" or upbringing is open to change. Transsexuality poses a direct challenge to this understanding.

First, it requires us to replace the simple nature/nurture dichotomy with a trichotomy because here we recognise the possibility of three things that might be at odds. Transsexuals are of one sex in their own opinion, though their bodies, together with the way they dress and behave, are all of the other sex. Transvestites, on the other hand, are frequently of one sex in their own opinion and in their bodily structure, but they have an urge to dress and behave in ways appropriate to the opposite sex. So we have three things: 1) personal opinion as to what one really is; 2) bodily features; 3) cultural factors, including what sex other people think one to be. As an aside one might note that given this complexity, it is all the more remarkable how generally stable and predictable is the relationship between symptomatic and constitutive features of sex.

Second, transsexuality upsets our ideas concerning what is or is not open to change. Let us accept for the moment that sex-change surgery really does succeed in altering a body of one sex to a body of the opposite sex. This would show that the physical is not as unchangeable as has been thought. Likewise, if a person dresses and behaves as a member of the opposite sex then new acquaintances will tend to treat him/her as a member of the symptomatic sex, although long-standing acquaintances would most likely have grave difficulties adjusting to the change. So the cultural is partly changeable, partly resistant (more or less) to change.

More generally, people seeking sex-change surgery pose a problem for medical ethics just because it is not clear anteced-ently that someone who is in full possession of their faculties might want to change their sex. We cannot without further ado say that the problem of whether such surgery should be per-formed in a particular case is not a doctor's problem, but just a patient's problem. There are ethical problems here, as the follow-ing example will make clear. Suppose a doctor considers such surgery purely cosmetic and altogether removed from the realms of curative medicine. You say, in effect, "I am a mere technol-ogist, like a builder. I will do the job I am asked to do as well as possible. But it is not my concern to determine whether or not this is a good idea, a cure for an illness or whatever. I might do a bit of 'counselling', but only so that the customer knows what to expect and will be happy enough with the finished result to pay my bill." If I wished to have my ears pierced I would seek out someone who has been properly trained and expect just such an attitude. I would not expect long consultations as to whether it would be good for me to have my ears pierced, nor would I expect the piercer to make the final decision about whether or not it should be done.

With regard to sex-changes, this stance is dubious for the following reason: we say "Let the customer beware" only in cases where the customer is indeed a rational adult, i.e. in full possession of his faculties. Is the demand for sex-change surgery the sort of demand that could be made by someone in full possession of his faculties? In particular, with a man who thinks he is a woman, is that thought not itself proof that in the relevant respect he is not in possession of his faculties? How could you come to believe he is right in thinking he is really a woman?

Suppose you decide that he is quite correct but this does not create any call for surgery. If the right analogy is with cosmetic surgery then such a reaction makes sense (though it may not convince or be accepted by the patient). A woman who seeks to have a very faint moustache removed might well be told that this is unnecessary, that it is detectable only by intimates who may even find it rather sweet and charming, enhancing rather than detracting from her femininity. Although the woman in question may or may not accept this advice, it is perfectly reasonable. But what if the doctor says "Some men like women with penises . . . "? This is utterly ridiculous, but why? Most likely because possession of normal male genital organs is generally considered to be the most basic constitutive feature of maleness. It simply cannot be taken to be merely a misplaced symptom, which is what the cosmetic surgery/technologist approach must assume it to be. The absurdity of treating it simply as a misplaced symptom suggests that the patient's belief that he is a woman is not true. Even if it were true, would surgery be justified? After all, it is rather dubious whether surgery can indeed make a man into a woman and not just into a mutilated man.

There seems good reason to think that the patient's belief is false. What then is to be done? Consider someone with a different belief that does not accord with the facts; for instance one might believe oneself to be Napoleon. For someone who is not Napoleon, there is no way that the facts can be brought into line with the belief that he is Napoleon. Is this a problem about beliefs or a problem about facts? Is it merely unfortunate that in this case we are unable to tailor the facts to suit this person's belief?

Consider another person with a false belief: someone who thinks he is the Prime Minister. In this case it is not impossible, although it might be difficult, to alter the facts and make the belief true. Would this solve the patient's problem? Surely not. Somebody who thinks he is Prime Minister when he is not is very badly wrong. To have such a belief and it be false would indicate a pretty radical impairment of your capacity for forming beliefs. It is because of this that the problems of such a person are not solved simply by making him Prime Minister. Even though that would overcome the gap between this thought of his and the facts, it would not cure the failings that led to such bizarre misconceptions. Whether you regard being a woman as like being Prime Minister or as like being Napoleon (i.e. something that can be attained or something you have to be all along); whichever, it does seem that the surgery could not possibly cure a man who thinks he is a woman if his problem is just a mismatch between his beliefs and the physiological facts about him. Indeed, surgery might simply make things worse if it purports to be a cure but is not.

A possible approach would be to admit that the patient's belief is misaligned with the facts and take the misalignment to be symmetrical. That is, not simply to consider the patient as a normal, but deluded, man; rather to consider him to be suffering from a simple mismatch between his body and the sex he feels himself to be. With such a symmetry, neither being as it were absolutely right or wrong, the best therapeutic approach might be to change whichever is more easily adaptable. If surgery seems easier than altering the patient's belief than surgery would be the best treatment. If not, then some form of psychotherapy would be the best. But surgery does not completely alter the facts even if it seems the easier way. It is at least questionable whether a man who has undergone a sex-change operation has been changed into a woman. If being a woman is not attainable but rather something that you have to be all along then he has not become a woman. This being so, the misalignment between his belief and the facts will not have been solved.

A final rationale for sex-change surgery is possible, namely that of humouring the patient. Here the doctor's attitude would be somewhat as follows: "You have this belief and it is wrong. It is not made true by surgery nor, of course, does surgery alleviate all the serious defects in cognitive capacity that this belief indicates. But it may make you feel happier so we will give you the surgery to humour you." This is rather like the case of the charming old lady who in her senility came to believe that she was the Queen. The staff in her old-folks' home gave her a wooden sword and she was quite happy going round creating knights. If sex-change surgery does not truly effect a sex-change but does make otherwise unhappy people more happy then this might be a reasonable, ethically defensible approach.

It thus seems that we have four possible attitudes that a doctor could take toward someone seeking a sex-change operation. The first is to treat it as purely cosmetic, an attitude that seems hardly defensible in view of the misalignment between the patient's belief and the facts. At the opposite extreme from this is the second, whereby the doctor considers the patient to be suffering from a serious delusion. This could only be exacerbated by surgery which would reinforce the still wrong belief that he is a woman. Such a doctor must consider some form of psychotherapy to be the best treatment.

The other two attitudes fall between these extremes. Third is that which treats the mismatch between belief and body as symmetrical, changing whichever is more easily changed. The best therapy from this point of view will depend on two factors: 1) whether the patient's belief seems easier to change than his physiology, and 2) whether sex-change surgery really does change a man into a woman (or vice versa). The fourth and final attitude is that of humouring, and this is the only stance that might, defensibly, offer such surgery fairly readily to a large proportion of these patients. It is defensible however only if there is good reason to believe that sex-change surgery does succeed in making otherwise unhappy people happier.

The difference between these four approaches is not simply a matter of technical medical judgement. Medical judgement as to how to deal with somebody who says he is a woman in a man's body will depend on your views on the metaphysics of sexuality.

Mariology and "Romantic Feminism": A Critique

SARAH COAKLEY

In this essay I propose to provide a brief critique of what I shall term the "romantic feminism" of some current Catholic Mariology, and I shall be focusing especially on the work of Leonardo Boff.[1] The juxtaposition of "romantic" and "feminist" is of course advisedly paradoxical, and, as I hope to show, at least one side of Boff's Mariology is actually self-defeating on any other "feminist" grounds, despite all its good intentions. In order, however, to contextualize a "romantic feminist" Mariology amidst a range of other possible options, I shall devote the first, and indeed greater, part of my essay to a general introduction to feminism and Mariology. Here I shall outline a rough typology of different sorts of "feminism" as canvassed in the secular sphere, and then align these types with a concomitant range of available feminist Mariological options. Indeed, I think it could be said on this basis that Mariology provides a most revealing litmus test for the strength and type of a feminist commitment, whether Christian or post-Christian. I shall then turn, secondly, to a short, critical, analysis of Boff's alternative Mariology, and assess the nature of his "feminist" commitment.

1. Types of "feminism", types of Mariology

It is a commonplace of secular feminist literature to divide feminist theory into three broad types: "liberal", "radical", and "post-modern"; but recent works by Alison Jaggar and Rosemarie Tong[2] have usefully complexified this typology to include other categories: "Marxist", "socialist", "psychoanalytic", and "existentialist" for instance. It is important here, however, as with any typology, to underline that such types are "ideal" in the Weberian sense, i.e. heuristic constructs that real examples may well cut across. For the purposes of our task, then, let us maintain the three basic types already mentioned – liberal, radical, and post-modern – sketching their characteristic tenets, views of human nature, and attendant possible Mariologies. I shall then suggest that to do critical justice to the current range of "feminist" Mariological options, we may need to add two further "ideal" types: "socialist" feminism (which is harder to define) and a curious hybrid back-formation "romantic feminism", to which male theologians influenced by Carl Gustav Jung seem particularly prone.

* * *

Liberal feminism, first, then, as classically enunciated by Mary Wollstonecraft in the eighteenth century (*A Vindication of the Rights of Women*, 1792) or John Stuart Mill in the nineteenth (*On the Subjection of Women*, 1869) pleaded for the full equality, rationality and intellectual ability of women alongside men, and for their rightful opportunity to compete in the public, professional sphere. Betty Friedan's celebrated *The Feminine Mystique*, published in 1963,[3] actually did little but recapitulate the themes of this particular discussion, and if anything was more (unrealistically) sanguine in assuming that women could thus succeed in a man's realm through sheer dogged effort. The attendant view of human nature here, as Alison Jaggar highlights (*op. cit.*, pp.37 ff.), was supposedly sex*less*: it was an Enlightenment vision of *mental* equality – rational, individual, autonomous; to Professor Higgins' complaint "Why can't a woman be more like a man?" the answer was, "She would be, given the right educational and franchise rights". In some contrast, however, more recent liberal feminists, Carolyn Heilbrun, for instance, have appealed, again on grounds of equality, to a form of psychological "androgyny" for men and women alike. Here, unlike the Jungian type of "androgyny" that we shall examine in connection with "romantic feminism", there is (supposedly at least) no *prescription* of gender traits; men and women aim for equal liberation from what Heilbrun calls the "confines of the appropriate . . . a full range of experience [is] open to *individuals* [note the characteristic liberal term] who may, as women, be aggressive, as men tender."[4] Again, the emphasis here is on freedom of choice, as if one could easily *concoct*, by sheer effort of the will, a well-balanced mixture of personality traits without particular regard for social conditioning or expectations.

Now this liberal feminist ethos, with its stress on equal rights, choice and self-determination for women is clearly not one that readily combines with Mariological themes; there is slim exegetical base, if any, surely, for a professional Mary – no "Madonna of the briefcase". And yet the theme of Marian "autonomy" found in Rosemary Radford Ruether's work bears at least a residual "liberal" imprint. Mary makes a "free choice", we are told. "Mary does not consult Joseph, but makes her own decision." The cooperation between God and Mary here is said to be on equal terms – a "co-creatorship between God and humanity".[5] In a different, and delightfully backhanded way, the early work of Mary Daly also stresses the autonomy of the Virgin's pregnancy: here is a woman who is at least "not defined exclusively by her relationships with men".[6] Yet in the same work Daly is already more critically perceptive than Ruether about the potential patriarchal undertones of the Annunciation story. After all, the Virgin did not say, "I shall do what *I* want to", but uttered the *Fiat* – "Let it be done unto me according to *Thy* word." "The alleged 'voluntariness' of the imposed submission in Christian patriarchy," she remarks, "has turned women against ourselves . . . disguising and reinforcing the internalization process."[7]

In sum, developed liberal feminist Mariologies are not common, although it has been remarked by Barbara Corrado Pope, in her interesting study of the Marian revival in nineteenth-century France, that pockets of local Marian devotion in rural France, based on visionary appearances, could bring a new sense of "empowerment and autonomy" to the recipients of such visions (notably adolescent young women); and hence, she suggests, the need quickly to institutionalize such sites as Lourdes, to make Benediction a central rite in them, and so re-ensure, as she puts it, that "the Son upstaged the mother".[8]

Perhaps curiously, however, and secondly, we find more Mariological work (or should we call it deconstructive Mariology?) clustering around theological forms of *radical feminism*. In secular radical feminism, the liberal quest for equality within the boundary of existing social relations is abandoned, for culture and society are now seen as *intrinsically* patriarchal through and through ("Sex class is so deep as to be invisible", in the celebrated opening words of Shulamith Firestone's *The Dialectic of Sex*)[9]. Here women are seen as oppressed not only intellectually, through gender exploitation, but physically through sexual and medical theory and gynaecological practice. (Daly ranges Hindu suttee, Chinese foot-binding, African female circumcision and European witch-burning all alongside modern Western gynaecology.[10]) The attendant view of human nature in radical feminism thus shifts the emphasis onto the body, and onto a new *female* biological essentialism: stripped of false male projections of appropriate "femininity" women may in a separatist mode actualize their true potential as lovers and mothers, regaining theoretical and political control of their own bodies. The notion of "androgyny" in any sense comes under sharp critical fire here and is revealed as already politically laden, for, as Jagger puts it, being "'masculine' carries *benefits* that being 'feminine' does not".[11] Androgyny, in Adrienne Rich's words, "*fails* in the naming of differences"; it fails to acknowledge the *struggle* that is involved in countering women's oppression.[12] As Mary Daly has hilariously suggested, it is like "two distorted halves of a human being stuck together – something like John Wayne and Brigitte Bardot scotch-taped together – as if two *distorted* bodies could make a whole"; at best, then, the concept of androgyny should, in its drawing on traditional gender stereotypes, naturally "self-liquidate".[13]

The alternative, at least for some of the earlier radical feminists such as Jane Alpert, Adrienne Rich and Susan Griffin,[14] was a glorification of female biology and "natural" motherhood that (arguably) merely inverted the old stereotypes in favour of women. The "inner power" in women was said to be her "capacity to bear and nurture children" (Alpert), "the power inherent in female biology" (Rich), or a woman's closeness to "nature" (Griffin). And Mary Daly persistently asserts the "*native* talent and superiority of women".[15] The Mariological accompaniment to this radical and separatist stance is, I suggest, two-sided. On the one side there is a thoroughgoing deconstruction of traditional Mariology, in all its multivalence, as an elaborate set of projections of the "feminine" by and for men. Marina Warner's *Alone of All Her Sex* performs this task with considerable sympathy and historical care; her conclusions however are almost entirely negative. Mary is by definition an impossible ideal as Virgin *and* mother, and thus a crushing exemplar for real mothers: "She was 'feminine' perfection personified, and no other woman was in her league."[16] Warner has time, significantly, for both the themes of the *Mater Dolorosa* (the grieving Mary at the foot of the cross) and the *Mater Misericordiae* (the mother of mercy sheltering the faithful under her cloak) – central aspects of late medieval piety; for here Mary – even though *within* sexist gender stereotypes – becomes a symbol of compassion and love reaching out beyond the boundaries of justice. But Warner's overall judgment is dismissive, and based on the deconstruction of those stereotypes typical of a radical: the Virgin "will now recede into legend", she predicts in ending; she "will be emptied of moral significance".[17]

Warner's work does not of course share that other "radical" trait – the assertion of a (superior) female biology. But this *is* characteristic of what remains of Mariology in Mary Daly's more recent works: *Gyn/Ecology* (1979) and *Pure Lust* (1988). Outrageously funny as ever, Daly viciously lampoons traditional Mariology as "*male* femininity". "In the charming story of the Annunciation," she writes, "the angel Gabriel appears to the terrified young girl, announcing that she has been chosen to become the mother of God. Her response to this sudden proposal is totaled [sic] non-resistance ['Let it be done to me according to thy word']. Physical rape is not necessary when the mind/

will/spirit has already been invaded."[18] Or, in *Pure Lust*, Daly adds an even more explicit parallelism to rape. "Like all rape victims in male myths [Mary] submits joyously to this unspeakable degradation."[19]

The other side of Daly's Mariology, however, aligns with her female essentialism and concomitant avowal of goddess-worship; for she sees in traditional Mariology a safe male *control* of a goddess spirituality struggling to get out; the "natural (wild) state of femaleness" is tamed;[20] Mary is but "an aftershadow of the great Moon goddess Marian."[21] True to her love of alliteration, Daly surpasses even herself in this marvellous sentence: "Dutifully dull and derivative, drained of divinity, [Mary] merits the reward of perpetual paralysis in patriarchal paradise."[22] For Daly, then, the Assumption is no elevation of real (wild) woman; it is all part of the "rape of the goddess". But it is a peculiarly post-war, '50s manifestation thereof; as women were "badgered into housewifery" again after the war, the Assumption became official dogma, and this was no coincidence. "As Mary 'went up', women went down, without realizing it. The familiar tactic of reversal was in operation, and as women gazed heavenward at the feminine mystique personified – Mary the happy housewife gone home to heaven – they were in reality being herded into the Womb-tomb, the Home."[23]

A profound difference from Daly's negative polemics is found when we turn to the psychoanalytic *interest* in motherhood characteristic of French post-modernist feminism, especially the work of Julia Kristeva, whom I shall take as my exemplar here because of her explicit fascination with the figure of the Madonna. Whereas liberal feminism, as a type, asserted women to be *rationally* equal with men, and radical feminism asserted women to be essentially and biologically *superior*, post-modernist feminism abandons altogether the notion of a universal human (female) nature, and explicitly embraces epistemological relativism. What we call sexual identity, according to post-modernist feminism, is an effect of our "discourse"; it is the complex *relationship* between language, social institutions and individual consciousness ("subjectivity"), all constantly in flux, which has to be explored and exposed if we are to understand why women submit, on the whole compliantly, to patriarchal structures. Thus, on a post-modern understanding, there is no fixed view of human nature. But there are, under the strong influence of Lacan's reading of Freud, various psychoanalytic theories of how so-called "feminine" thought becomes marginalized and repressed in what French feminists call "phallocentric" society. For French feminism, then, as Chris Weedon puts it in her excellent *Feminist Practice and Post-Structuralist Theory*: "An understanding of how discourses of biological sexual differences are mobilized, in a particular society, at a particular moment, is the *first stage* in intervening in order to initiate change."[24]

In the thought of Julia Kristeva,[25] any idea of stasis or lurking biological essentialism is avoided by the insistence that feminists aim at no fixed or ideal state. "Woman" is *deconstructive* as a notion: it is not something static or definable; for it is that which the patriarchal "symbolic order" rejects, represses and marginalizes; and hence its meanings lie beyond "language and society". Kristeva distinguishes here what she calls the "symbolic order" and the "semiotic order". The former is the prevailing linguistic realm of order and objectivity, into which the child enters and is largely caught when it first learns to distinguish itself from its mother. (Kristeva here follows Lacan in underlining the importance of the so-called "mirror-phase", when the child first realizes, on seeing itself in the mirror, that it is a distinguishable person.) The latter realm, the "semiotic", is for Kristeva the link back into the "pre-Oedipal" phase of "primary narcissm", i.e. identification with the mother. But it is also the seat of subversive creativity, which may flash out in music, poetry or other forms of writing which release repressed material from the unconscious. Such writing has no *intrinsic* connection with the female body or libido; at all points Kristeva wards off the possibility of an essentialist interpretation, and hence her insistence that "woman [i.e., in any fixed form] *as such* does not exist".[26]

What is more interesting for our Mariological purposes, however, is Kristeva's view that it is not so much "woman" but *motherhood* that is repressed in our patriarchal society. In two important articles, "Héréthique de l'amour", translated as "Stabat Mater",[27] and "Motherhood according to Giovanni

Bellini",[28] Kristeva uses reflection on the symbols and iconography of traditional Marian devotion to argue a complex thesis. First (in "Stabat Mater"), she proposes that the idea of the "virginal maternal" was a way of dealing with what she calls "*feminine* paranoia" (i.e. not just a set of male fantasies fobbed off onto woman, as is more commonly claimed). It may reflect, for instance, a "paranoid" lust for female power in the vision of the heavenly queen;[29] or else what Kristeva calls the "paranoid logic" of the deposition scene – "the 'wrenching' between desire for the masculine corpse and negation of death".[30] But in any case, the wholesale rejection of Marian mythology by mainstream feminism leaves a gap, according to Kristeva, a felt need to express some of the dynamics of motherhood which she feels remain unvoiced by "avant-garde" feminists. What about the implicit "war" between mother and daughter in the daughter's production of a first child, she asks? Or the "corporeal and psychological suffering of childbirth", which may be disowned or shrugged off by a feminist superwoman?[31]

Again, and further, in her complex essay on Bellini's huge production of Madonna paintings, Kristeva ingeniously hypothesizes a development in Bellini's (male) attitude to maternity, his various attempts – according to her – to probe back behind the "primal repression" which results from the child's *objectivizing* of the mother.[32] In both these Marian essays Kristeva suggests that it is the return to a "primary narcissism" (i.e. the supposed original identification of a child with the mother) which somehow makes the thought of *death* bearable.[33] If this *is* so, then motherhood is certainly in need of a (profound) new discourse, yet somehow one that escapes the traps and "paranoid" distortions that feminism has highlighted. And there are also the dangers of the so-called "phallic mother" – the over-dominating or subsuming maternal figure – whom Kristeva has been herself accused of insufficiently guarding against.[34]

If Kristeva's post-modern feminism attempts to shift the interest back to mothering, whilst substantially deconstructing the virginal motherhood of traditional dogma, *socialist feminism* is for different reasons also concerned with the social construction of motherhood. We need to include a brief look here at socialist feminism in our typology because of its easy alignment with liberation theology, and its interest in the economic and political basis of women's struggle against patriarchy. According to Alison Jaggar, one of socialist feminism's most sophisticated exponents, socialist feminism is actually a critical amalgam of various feminist strands.[35] But its central intention, as I read it, is to revise and correct what Jaggar calls "traditional" Marxist feminism, which sees woman's oppression as precisely residing in her exclusion from *public* production. This Jaggar sees as a simplistic and "gender-blind" diagnosis; for there are specific forms of female oppression which even the right ordering of the workplace would not alleviate. A woman's "alienation" arises not just from the class structures of capitalism, which also alienate men, but from imposed cultural alienations which are gender-specific: alienation from her own body, for instance, through false expectations about sexuality and motherhood. Thus Jaggar argues that contemporary childbearing practices ultimately estrange mothers from their own children, establishing an "extreme mutual dependence" through which the individual mother finds her meaning and social recognition, but which is then doomed to be painfully repudiated in her children's adolescence. The underlying problem, in Jaggar's view, is that "The social relations of contemporary motherhood make it impossible for [the mother] to see the child as a *whole person*, part of a larger community to which both mother and child belong."[36]

I cite those (rather sophisticated) views of Jaggar in brief résumé, because they make interesting comparison with what might be called the socialist feminist *rhetoric* of some recent Mariology from the liberationist camp. This is, for instance, another side of Rosemary Ruether's interpretation of Lukan Mariology, and especially of the Magnificat. "Luke's liberation language," she claims, "is explicitly economic and political. The mighty are put down from their thrones; the rich are sent empty away."[37] In this, Mary, a woman, "embodies and personifies the oppressed and subjugated *people*";[38] for "it is women especially who represent the Church by calling others out of bondage into freedom. The despised woman as the poorest of the poor has symbolic priority in the Church."[39] A similar line is taken by

Ivone Gebara and Maria Clara Bingemer, fellow Brazilians of
Boff, in their recent *Mary, Mother of God, Mother of the Poor*.[40]
Their avowed method can appropriately be called "socialist feminist", for it is non-essentialist ("closely connected to the historical moment in which we are living"), and devoted to "the awak-
ening of the other half of humankind, the women's half, to living
realities from which they have been alienated."[41] But like Ruether, Gebara and Bingemer pursue the liberationist theme of the
Magnificat in such a way that Mary here becomes merely a type
of the *poor*: "It is on the basis of her poverty and unimportance
[besides her moral virtues and human qualities] that God sows
in her the seed of the liberation of a whole people."[42] My point
here is that the specific cutting edge of socialist feminism such
as Jaggar's is completely lost if the "gender specific" forms of
alienation she wants to highlight (in contradistinction from more
"traditional" Marxist feminism) are lost sight of. Thus it is not
clear to me that using Mary as a type of the poor is a *bona fide
feminist* ploy; it may be a highly effective liberationist one – but
is it specifically to do with women? Worse, in its identification
of woman with the "poorest of the poor" (Ruether), or with
"poverty and unimportance" (Gebara and Bingemer), may it
not also unwittingly be signalling a form of (divine) compliance
with this state of affairs? We shall find these paradoxes reiterated
in one side of Boff's Mariology, indeed the more subversive side,
which even then, I shall argue, is not truly "feminist" in any
accepted secular sense. To Boff's *Maternal Face of God* we now
turn, then, for a brief résumé and critique – and for an analysis
of his vision of the "feminine other".

2. Leonardo Boff and "romantic feminism"

I have gone to such lengths to typologize secular "feminisms"
and their possible accompanying Mariologies in order to show,
I fear, how weak-kneed is Boff's supposed commitment to "feminism" in comparison. And yet, because Boff is in Roman Cath-

olic terms a potential subersive who has already suffered one public remonstrance from Cardinal Ratzinger, *The Maternal Face of God* is a book that is presumed to be, indeed marketed as, "innovative", "feminist", and in touch with the latest relevant news from the "social sciences".[43]

I want to argue that there are two sides to this book, existing in paradoxical relationship, but neither of them genuinely "feminist" in any of the senses we have so far discussed. One side, which occupies most of the book, represents the hybrid back-formation which I suggest we call "romantic feminism", involving a construction of the "feminine other" which has its roots in Romanticism, and which in fact provides only a thinly-disguised reorientation of traditional gender stereotypes. The other side of Boff's book, sneaked into chapter 12, "Mary, Prophetic Woman of Liberation", is actually a quite strongly subversive bit of ecclesiology from a liberation perspective, hung on a meditation about the Magnificat. But again, as with Ruether and Gebara/Bingemer, this is not, as far as I can see, significantly *feminist*, i.e. gender-specific about women's fears of alienation and oppression, as opposed to the more inclusive oppression of the poor in general. The mixture of these two sides of Boff's book may actually, I acknowledge, be extremely clever in the context and constraints in which he is operating politically in the Roman Catholic Church. That is, his romantic "feminism", while sounding vaguely titillating, is actually point for point closely in line with recent papal pronouncements on Mary,[44] and not likely to cause trouble; whilst his more revolutionary message is smuggled in secondarily, and harnessed to the intensive emotive power of South American Marian devotion. Be that as it may, it is his construction of the "feminine other", his "romantic feminism", which I now want to look at coolly and critically.

* * *

Despite some "liberal" feminist-sounding statements at the beginning of Boff's book, rejecting the "domination" and "subjugation" of women by men, Boff seems unclear about whether he actually seeks women's equality (which, incidentally, Pope John

Paul II does explicitly purport to!).⁴⁵ Rather, the sexes for Boff are said to be reciprocal or "complementary".⁴⁶ Underlying this is what amounts to a form of biological essentialism, and a persistent failure to distinguish clearly between physical sex on the one hand (male and female) and societal gender expectations on the other ("masculine" and "feminine"). Hormones, for instance, he says significantly "determine" "masculine" and "feminine" behaviour.⁴⁷ Thus, despite an early section (in chapter 3) in which Boff indicates some awareness of the critical discussion of the problems of sex and gender (although the only noted secular feminist he has read is de Beauvoir),⁴⁸ it becomes clear later on that an *a priori* and quite uncritical acceptance has been made of Jung's theory of "androgyny".⁴⁹ According to this theory (to be carefully distinguished from the "liberal" theory of free choice in androgynous characteristics discussed earlier), both men and women encompass so-called "masculine" and "feminine" traits; but Jung is notoriously lopsided and prescriptive in the way he enunciates the theory of a woman's "animus" (her "masculine" element) in comparison with a man's "anima". Not only does he accept that these gender stereotypes are given, and that a man ought to be *primarily* "masculine" (or a woman "feminine"); but his account of a man's "anima" is infinitely more subtle and variable in its positive possibilities than is his vision of a woman's "animus", on which he has mostly caustic things to say. Thus he can utter such remarks as:

> In men, Eros, the function of relationship, is usually less developed than Logos. In women, on the other hand, Eros is an expression of their true nature, while their Logos is often a regrettable accident.⁵⁰

The strong implicit sexism of Jung's theory of the self has been well exposed by critics such as Naomi Goldenberg;⁵¹ but Boff is blissfully unaware of such feminist critiques of Jung, and indeed goes on to repeat all the same Jungian mistakes. Thus he assumes certain qualities to be "feminine" ("life, depth, mystery, tenderness, interiority, and caring",⁵² or – elsewhere – Marian "humility" and "discretion"⁵³). He then hypostatizes these characteristics, and shrouds them in an appropriately apophatic obscurity. The romantic heritage of his thought becomes clear in all this: "*das ewig Weibliche* (the eternal Feminine) leading us [i.e. men] on and upwards". Boff makes this explicit by his approving quotation from Evdokimov: "In the human being, the religious principle is expressed by woman."[54]

I think it will be clear by now that what Boff calls "feminism" is actually the appropriation, within a masculinist framework, of certain qualities normatively and prescriptively associated with women. No wonder then that "we" in this book means "we men". The "feminine other" is a male construct. Hence the revealing remarks in his conclusion: "Through the feminine *we* make ourselves capable of another kind of relationship, more communal, more tender, more in solidarity with our roots in cosmos and earth. All great human beings [men again?], all profoundly integrated personalities, have been gentle spirits who have valued the expressions of the anima."[55]

Unsurprisingly, this theory of the integration of the "feminine other" finds its metaphysical counterpart in the appropriation of Mary into the Trinity by virtue of her special relationship to the ("feminine") Spirit. Again, Jung is followed verbatim, in his theory that the Marian dogmas of the '50s implicitly allowed the Virgin into the Godhead, and turned the otherwise lopsided Trinity into a balanced "quaternity"[56] – though Boff adjusts this slightly in order to avoid the suggestion that he is actually invoking a fourth person. (There would otherwise, of course, also be an equal balance of "masculine" and "feminine" in the Godhead.) Indeed Mary is seen as "definitively united to the Spirit"; "Mary's eschatological actualization of the feminine . . . reigns through the Holy Spirit at the very heart of the Trinity."[57]

I have elsewhere provided a sustained criticism of a similar (well-meaning) shift to a "feminine" Holy Spirit in the work of Yves Congar;[58] but it will be clear enough by now what the problems are: whilst Father and Son remain central to the events of salvation and resolutely and prescriptively reaffirmed as "masculine", how much does it really concede to attribute "femininity" to the notoriously neglected pneumatological principle?

Only in the extraordinarily different tone of chapter 12, where Mary becomes a "prophetic woman of liberation", does Boff conclude that a woman, Mary, could appropriately evidence strength and determination, characteristics of the "revolutionary". But our sense that this might at last signal a departure from the Jungian disapproval of the female "animus" is instantly undercut by the realization that here Mary stands not really for womanhood but for "an oppressed *people* – who long for a voice in society and liberation from its evils".[59]

Conclusion

Let me now sum up. I have tried to show that the sort of "feminism" espoused by Boff and other male theologians influenced especially by Jung and the earlier romantic views on "androgyny" that underlie him – though well-intentioned and in some respects ground-breaking in conservative Roman Catholic circles – limps well behind critical thinking in the secular feminist sphere, and is representative only of a partially informed masculinist perspective. Moreover a wide range of Mariological options other than those suggested by "romantic feminism" are already at least fragmentarily in play in the available feminist theological literature, aligning themselves with the major types of secular feminist theory. If most of these options have so far been negative critiques of traditional Mariology, this in itself is a highly illuminating exercise, and the fact of this critique does not mean, as Kristeva has indicated, that the fascination with the events of maternity is likely to disappear. Hence there is the remaining need, as Boff himself charmingly acknowledges, for *women* now to develop new philosophical theories of motherhood, new symbolizations of the maternal. For these, Boff rightly says, will surely be "shaped very differently" from men's, and will involve, if I am right, a telling deconstruction of the notion of the "feminine other".[60]

The Dark Knowing of Morgan Le Fay: Women, Evil and Theodicy

MARY GREY

Introduction

In this paper I am approaching the question of theodicy – that is, the justification of God in the face of evil and suffering – from an aspect ignored by traditional theodicies, namely, the scapegoating of women as responsible for sin and evil. First of all, I want very briefly to expose the lack of gender awareness within traditional theodicies; secondly, I discuss through a journey into mythology, namely, through the re-telling of the story of the "demonic" Morgan Le Fay from the Arthurian legends, the complexity of Christianity's encounter with paganism as "otherness"; thirdly, I use the metaphor of "dark knowing" to explore evil on the basis of a philosophy of connection. What this calls for is a new naming of good and evil, and corresponding images of the Divine, which sheds light on how God is present to the believer in the face of suffering and evil.

Gender awareness and traditional theodicy

There are four central ways of responding to the theodicy question. The first – an approach belonging to classical Hinduism – is to assert that evil is an illusion, as is the whole physical world.

This inherently dualist view has had the consequence of failing adequately to struggle against social evils – as these would also belong to the realm of illusion. The origins of dualism present problems for feminist theology. Some feminists believe that the good/evil dichotomy is one which feminist theology should reject. It is the underlying error of patriarchal thinking that the dialectics of human existence, for example, the oppositions of male/female, human/non-human nature, body/spirit are all understood to be good/evil dualisms. And because these dualisms scapegoat the evil side as female, *sexism is seen as the underlying foundation of the good/evil ideology*.[1]

The second approach is to understand evil as *privatio boni*, or deprivation of the good (the position of the early Augustine). So sin, disease and evil have no independent existence: they are rather a defect in the natural order. This position avoids dualism, and has a certain logic in that, according to Aristotle, every virtue implies its vice as corollary, but does it do adequate justice to the sheer overwhelming force of evil, and the fact that, existentially, we experience evil as a distinctive, destructive power?

Thirdly, Augustine, as is well known, explained evil through the sin of human disobedience, which was a direct consequence of the flawed human will.[2] It is a deeply pessimistic view, because Adam was a microcosm of the entire human race:

> . . . humanity produced, what humanity became, not what it was when created, but when, having sinned, it was punished. (*City of God*, 13.3)

But Augustine, though explaining the first sin of our parents, has simply removed the theodicy question one stage further back: why did human beings choose evil? Why was the will flawed? Why did he not see that his views would legitimate the authority of Imperial Church, the dominance of man over woman, free person over slave? In the explanation given by Elaine Pagels, it was better to be guilty than helpless – to believe that disaster and suffering were the wages of sin, rather than part of the inevitable rhythms of nature.[3] Further, through the principle of harmony, Augustine was able to reconcile what appeared to be evil with the harmony of the total picture – which we cannot see.

Of the many difficulties with this idea of punishment for dis-obedience, the most catastrophic one for justice in the world is the fact that the inflicting of pain becomes ethical. Since God who is omniscient and perfect inflicts pain as punishment, what is wrong with that? *Suffering and the inflicting of pain are not seen as ethical abuse.*

This argument is linked with the fourth type of theodicy, which is a kind of "God the Pedagogue" theodicy, favoured by John Hick, Richard Swinburne and popularised in many works of spirituality. In its simplest form it is that we learn by our mis-takes; suffering is the way we become mature human beings, capable of relationship with God. Evil is here real and useful. Witness C.S. Lewis's explanations of his wife's terrible sufferings:

> But is it credible that such extremities of torture should be necessary for us? Well, take your choice. The tortures occur. If they are unnecessary, there is no God or a bad one. If there is a good God, then these tortures are necessary. For no even moderately good Being could possibly inflict or permit them if they weren't.[4]

There have been many critiques of this theodicy on the grounds that it removes final redemption to the meta-historical level, it devalues the physical realities of life (what is truly human is what separates us from the physical), but most of all because of the concept of God involved. As Dorothee Soelle cried:

> Who wants such a God? Who gains anything from him? Every expla-nation that looks away from the victim and identifies itself with a righteousness that is supposed to stand behind the suffering, has already taken a step in the direction of theological sadism, which wants to understand God as the torturer.[5]

"Through the Devil's Gateway"

It is important to be clear about the ways in which women have been associated with evil by the Christian tradition. There have been three main ways – through denigration of the female body and its functions, through the supposed demonic forces at work in the female subconscious, and specifically through the scapegoating of women through myths of the Fall.[6]

Fear of and disgust at the female body has a clear history in both Judaism and Christianity up till the present day. Jean-Paul Sartre, for example, identified the female body with holes and slime, found female sexuality obscene and the sex act the castration of man. What is not so well understood is the corollary that the rejection of the female body becomes a form of sanctity, seen in the extremes of body-rejecting asceticism of the women saints, and the glorification of the Virgin Mary as *virgo intacta*, seen as bodily integrity, a "closed gate", and therefore a return to the pre-Fall state of innocence.

Secondly, the demonic forces working through the female unconscious follows from the Jungian identification of a distinct "masculine" *animus* and "feminine" *anima* as recognisable personality types. But the "feminine" is frequently ambiguous and identified with darker forces. Woman's body is seen as the dark continent. (For example, think of the stereotype of the "devouring mother".) Therefore, it is a feminist task to contextualise the myths in their real life situations with all their ambiguities.[7] Thirdly, a feminist analysis is often focused on the wounding or loss of women's self-esteem under patriarchy. But this wounding is at the level of the damaged consciousness of the symbols and images emerging from the depths of the psyche. Hence, *the "demonic knowing" of Morgan Le Fay as part of our cultural heritage needs to be unmasked by tracking it to its cultural origins and asking whether another truth can be disclosed.*

1. Morgan Le Fay – sorceress or shaman?

Scapegoated for sin and the Fall, linked with bodily weakness and inferiority, the feminine unconscious seen as "dark" and "evil" – how can women find a way out of these mazes of ambiguity? How can we construct a pedagogy of good and evil which comes to terms honestly with human responsibility for evil, seeking neither to blame God nor to scapegoat women?

First, we have to find a better way of naming good and evil, a framework which is more adequate to hold the terrible weight and complexity of suffering which overwhelms so many people and societies. From this new naming it must be made clear why certain images of God are inadequate both to explain evil and to transform and eradicate it.

Secondly, we seek to delve to the roots of the scapegoating. The question will be: is it possible, when pursuing evil to its rootedness in historical contexts in all their particularity and specificity, to see that the projecting of evil on to women made certain situations "tolerable" for those in power, justifying certain actions?

Seeking to do this through the old myths which pre-date the coming of Christianity and Judaism – be these of Egyptian, Greek or Celtic origin – the tension will become very clear between what was thought to be acceptable as "Christian" and what ought to be rejected as "pagan".[8] The clash is particularly sharp in the story of Morgan Le Fay, Morgaine, Daughter of the Lake – as her name means – who is actually in an earlier form known as Modron, the Celtic Earth Mother, and linked with Morrigan, the Irish Goddess. Vital for this investigation of the association of women with evil is the fact that her story is linked with the legend of King Arthur, the Once and Future King. The ever-growing cult of Arthurian legend, the Quest for the Holy Grail and the growth of Glastonbury as a centre of Christian pilgrimage and New Age spirituality have also stimulated interest in Morgan Le Fay. These have discovered an alternative interpretation behind Arthurian myth, which normally portrays her as an evil sorceress plotting the destruction of Arthur and his Christian knights and rejecting all that is Christian, good and holy.

As I engage in a re-telling of the story of Morgaine (Morgan Le Fay), I do so in intentional awareness of a feminist, postmodern perspective, aware of the multiplicity and particularity of sources, Celtic and pre-Christian, mediaeval, pan-European and Eastern, Victorian and neo-Victorian, as well as of Goddess and New Age spiritualities which all have their own perspective, interpretation and vested interests in the Arthurian legends and the search for the Holy Grail. Although my own perspective is also limited, it breaks ground in asking new questions. I make no claim to discover the "real truth" of Morgaine – such an attempt is illusory – but I hope that in struggling with the questions raised by the re-telling, understanding will be gained as to how human beings cope with evil.

This re-telling of the story of Morgaine[9] situates itself within the generally-accepted historical context of the Arthurian legend in post-Roman Britain. Central to the legend's power is the unique place which Glastonbury holds in the religious history of Britain. Here it was, so the story goes, that Joseph of Arimathea came, after the death of Christ, bearing the Chalice of the Last Supper. Where he and his faithful companions rested was known as Weary-All Hill; where he planted his staff blossomed the famous Glastonbury thorn, which flowers at Christmas time. (Indeed, this still blossoms today – though it has been replanted – a rare thorn which is usually found in the Levant.)

The Chalice which he brought was to be the source of the mediaeval quest for the Holy Grail, the unifying force of Arthur's fellowship of the Round Table. But even before the founding of any monastic settlement at Glastonbury – which could have been around the fourth century – it was as the Lake-Isle of Avalon, Isle of Apples, Lake-Village, that its significance grew. Avalon is certainly one of the most sacred sites of the world: some would say it has mystical and astrological significance.[10] Certainly, before Glastonbury had any importance the religion of the Great Mother and of the Druids flourished at Avalon. It is as the great Priestess of Avalon, together with the ancient shaman Merlin – whose involvement with the Arthurian legends is but a moment in a more complex history – that we should imagine Morgaine. As Monica Sjoo tells us:

> On the sacred island of Avalon, Apple Island, Morgan Le Fay ("the fairy") ruled over nine sisters, and taught how plants can be used to

cure illness . . . She was one of the many renowned shamans, practic-
ing ancient wisdom on an enchanted island.[11]

But Morgan Le Fay, Wise Woman, Healer, with authority over
her people is transformed by the Christian legends into a vile
sorceress and temptress, incestuous lover of Arthur, symbol both
of female degraded sexuality as well as obstacle to the success of
the Knights on their quest. This is a familiar theme in patriarchal
legend – Dido was an obstacle for Aeneas, Ariadne for Theseus:
it is a well worn theme.

So, as the old story is retold, central will be these questions:
First, what is it about Christian understanding of good and evil
which demanded the rejection of the older religion? Secondly,
why are women scapegoated within it as evil – it is almost
impossible in the whole of the Arthurian cycle for women to
discover "usable" stories – and why is this identification unchallenged? Thirdly, Christianity's strength has often been in adopt-
ing or creatively transforming certain traditions of the older
religions: what ethical norms, and epistemological pre-suppo-
sitions governed the adoption of certain aspects and the exclusion
of others? Fourthly, does the demonization of Morgaine tell us
anything about the way society treats the discourse of minorities?
Finally, what concept of God arises from a new understanding
of evil?

2. The coming of Arthur

Just as the spread of Christianity to Western Europe began with
the need for military victory – the Emperor Constantine in AD
312 being told through the vision of the Cross in the sky, "By
this sign you will conquer" so it was in Britain: King Oswald
of Northumbria before his fiercest battle against the pagan King,
Penda, had a similiar vision.[12] But a hundred years before this
– in the fifth century – Britain was facing a greater crisis. The
Romano-British "culture" was breaking up, as Rome was
threatened with invasions from Goths, Huns and Vandals. But
even the Pax Romana had been precariously built on fragile and

temporary truces with the ancient British tribes. "They create a desolation and they call it peace", as the Roman historian Tacitus cynically described his own nation through the words of a Caledonian chieftain.[13] Now the peril was greater still, as the Saxons began to invade and the threat of further Viking invasions loomed large.

Against this background a plan appears to have been conceived that a great King should be born, capable of holding the loyalty of the ancient Celtic tribes as well as the dominant Romano-British forces, and to unite them both against the Saxons. The hope was to give the country relief from war and violence.

The source of the plan – according to Dolores Ashcroft Nowicki – was really the Great Mother of Celtic spirituality herself, in association with Merlin (or Taliessin in some sources, variously Wise Man, Shaman and poet-musician), who served the Great Mother, (in Celtic religion the Lady of Sorrows, the Giver of Life and Death). It is not unusual in pre-patriarchal religions to find a divine couple, the Great Mother and her consort, wielding authority together.

The child's mother would be Igraine, also priestess-trained in Avalon, sister to Viviane, Lady of the Lake, and married to Gorlois, Duke of Cornwall. Morgaine is their daughter, known as Morgause in other legends. The child's father was to be Uther Pendragon, High King of Britain. As the same source explains it:

> The value of Igraine's participation is her blood line, linking her to the ancient Sea-Kings of the Drowned Lands (Atlantis, or the lost Kingdom of Lyonesse), the oldest royal line of the West. To join such a lineage with that of Uther Pendragon was to plan the creation of a dynasty of enormous power, both temporal and spiritual. The child of such a pairing would be the Once and Future King whose coming had been planned by the Goddess for many centuries.[14]

But there was a deeper reason than the political or military challenge. Marion Zimmer Bradley depicts the fears of the Celtic and Ancient British people that the coming of Christianity with its exclusive Father-God, would mean the suppression of the older religion, the denial of the Mother. Hence, in her rewriting of the story, Glastonbury, the Isle of Priests, symbolises Christianity and its hatred of paganism, and Avalon is the heart of the old religion. In fact, geographically, Glastonbury and Avalon are the same place, but Avalon can only be approached by summoning the magic barge through the mists – in other words, through an altered consciousness, an ability to "see" things differently. And the dangers are real that, as Christianity conquers, Avalon will disappear forever into the mists, its worship, rituals, healing powers and Goddess wisdom vanished forever. This has already happened to the Fairy People, the Little Dark People (the indigenous Celts?) who have already melted to oblivion, although it is suggested that, through her name, Morgaine of the Fairies, she must be descended from them. The tension between Glastonbury and Avalon is sharpened precisely where it affects women:

> Glastonbury has denied Avalon, denied the Mother, the Goddess. "There is no Goddess", for the principle of woman, so they say, is the principle of all evil.[15]

And this is why the two worlds are drifting apart: the world of the Christians, with One God and the Christ, and beside it and behind it, the world where the Great Mother still rules . . . where the Old People have chosen to live and worship:

> To most men our world is now lost in the midst of the Summer Sea.[16]

My interest here is the link between the suppression of the Goddess religion and consequent scapegoating of women as responsible for evil, sharply focused by the Glastonbury/Avalon tension, and the way Christianity has failed to sever the supposed link between women and evil, and where it is itself a dominant religion failing to recognize and learn from the wisdom of minority groups.

Avalon, then, planned the birth of the royal Child to solve a political crisis and to avoid the threat of religious oblivion. Because of his mother, Ygraine, he would be true to the Holy Mysteries of Avalon. Through his father he would command the allegiance of the armies of Britain. Even if Christianity became stronger, he would defend the right of the Old People to worship the Mother in peace. To this end he would be given the Holy Regalia of Avalon – the Cup, Sword (Excalibur) and the Lance. Thus what in the mediaeval legends of Europe – as told by Chretien de Troyes and Wolfram von Eschenbach, for example[17] – and in the Perceval legends, are seen as Christian symbols, are here given a more ancient origin.

What suggests that actual historical events lie behind this story is that the plan went astray. Originally, what Merlin had planned was that he would spirit away the child on his birth and bring him to Avalon to be schooled by Merlin in the ways of the Mother. This did not work. The problem was that Igraine was still married to Gorlois. There had to be a gigantic subterfuge to engineer the union of Igraine with Uther Pendragon, who masqueraded as Gorlois in his absence. But Gorlois was killed in battle:

> the death of Gorlois was not part of Merlin's scheme and . . . this one event was the basic flaw that was to mar the whole plan. Otherwise the child could easily have been passed off as Gorlois's until the birth . . . But Gorlois was slain and too many people had seen him killed at the same time that he was "seen" in the Queen's chamber. There was no way round it, the child was known to be Uther's, but born out of wedlock . . . a "bastard" as indeed was Merlin himself.[18]

So Arthur was born, half-brother to Morgaine, who from the first had an unusual relationship with him. Contemporary knowledge of developmental psychology would ask how it must affect the emotional development of a little girl, whose father is murdered in order that her mother re-marry, whose stepfather has no interest in her, to be given charge of this special boy-child through and beyond life itself.

From many sources it is known that Morgaine became associated with Avalon from an early age – all the Great Mother traditions seem to concentrate on her. Hence her cooperation in the second fateful step of the story – the making of the Sacred Marriage with Arthur himself, the famous doomed incestuous union, has a ring of inevitability. This was a practice known to many ancient religions:

> ... the young and virginal princess was dedicated from birth to the service of the Goddess. She would have been called, as were the priestesses of the Temple of Naradek in ancient Atlantis, to walk, accompanied only by the High Priest of the Rite, the dark, lonely way between the House of the Virgins and the sacred Grove where the Rite and an unknown priest of the Old Religion awaited her. She would have returned in the early light of dawn, a maid no more but "something far greater". The future mother of one destined to be not just a teacher and friend of kings, but one whose very name would be part of Britain's heritage.[19]

This was the Sacred Marriage as well as the King-making of Arthur. (Merlin himself had been the product of such a union.) The story of Arthur's King-making is linked, secondly, with the ancient fertility-rite of the killing of the King Stag and subsequent marriage with the Virgin Huntress.

But if ever a union was ill-fated it was this one. From the incestuous coupling – the sources vary as to the degree of complicity or ignorance of the two involved – came Gwydion/Mordred, who would deliver the fatal wound to Arthur, bringing about the collapse of his dreams of a united Britain, and the fellowship of the Round Table.

But this lay still in the future: the story unfolds with the solemn bestowal of the Sacred Regalia of Avalon on Arthur by the Lady of the Lake. The significance of this is that Arthur is now consecrated to the values of the religion of the Mother. Reaching for the sword, Arthur was prevented from doing so by the Lady of the Lake until he had sworn to be loyal to the Goddess and traditions of Avalon. He is persuaded by Merlin that to participate in Christian Eucharist does not involve betraying the Goddess – an exercise in inter-faith somewhat incredible to contemporary sensitivities.

The tragedy is now set in motion by the devotion of Arthur's beloved wife Guinevere (Gwenhwyfar) to Christianity – a devotion totally hostile to Avalon, Morgaine and all she stands for.

It is she who persuades Arthur to fight under the banner of the Cross in a decisive battle against the Saxons, forsaking the Dragon banners of Ancient Britain, thus losing the loyalties of the old tribes. So Arthur has betrayed Avalon, and Viviane, the Lady of the Lake, comes to the Court at Caerleon to accuse him of this betrayal. The Feast of Pentecost had become for Arthur the special occasion for the Companions of the Table to gather, show loyalty and celebrate their fellowship. But, in the very act of accusing Arthur of betrayal, the priestess of Avalon – according to this version of the story – is cut down savagely and murdered. Morgaine's outrage at her death is worsened by Arthur's refusal to allow her burial at Avalon – she is taken to the Abbey at Glastonbury. Again and again will the theme recur of the need for women to repent, since they are more responsible for sin in the first place.

But the scheming of Morgaine must be seen in a different light. Scheming it certainly is: she plots against Arthur to achieve the return of Excalibur to Avalon. She even plots the death of Arthur – as traitor – to be replaced by Accolon, Druidic priest and her lover. Our question must be: is the rightness or wrongness affected by the fact that in context the worshippers of the old religion must struggle for identity, against betrayal, their values, skills and rituals cursed as magic and sorcery? Is it not the case that those who are in an oppressed and dominated situation have to resort to scheming and manipulation for sheer survival?

The climax of the drama comes – in a theme already immortalised by Wagner – in the passage of the Holy Grail from the earth. Morgaine and the old Priestess, Raven, have come to Arthur's court to recover the Holy Regalia for Avalon. As the people gather for Mass, Morgaine hears that they are to use the Sacred Cup. Then she knows what she must do. She summons the Goddess to preserve the Sacred Cup, the cauldron of Ceridwen:

> She felt the rushing downward of power, felt herself standing taller, taller, as the power flooded through her body and soul and filled her; she was no longer conscious of Raven's hands holding her upright,

filling her, like the chalice, with the sacred wine of the holy presence . . . [20]

And so Morgaine, Morgan Le Fay, took the Holy Cup, glowing like a jewel (some said shining like a star) and moved among the company giving them to drink of the Holy Presence. Some said they had been filled with good things from the cauldron of Ceridwen herself. Finally, she drank herself, tasting the sweet water from the Sacred Well.

Now came the Great Magic: now the Hall was filled by a rushing wind, and great flapping wings were heard. The altar was bare – and the Cup was gone. The Grail would not be found again on this earth, although the great Quest to find it was now afoot among Arthur's knights, the Quest that would inspire literature and legend from now on. Indeed this was the final irony: although Arthur had forsaken the Goddess, and she had scattered his fellowship, yet her last and holiest of visions had inspired the most passionate legend of Christian worship.

Although this passage is an intertwining of many themes – the conflict between Avalon and Glastonbury, the longing for the priesthood and ministry of women to be recognized, the linking of Grail Cup and Eucharistic chalice with the sacramental richness of creation – it also offers insight to one of my initial questions: the nature of the dichotomy between Christianity and the paganism it abhorred. For the mediaeval legends as we know them, as well as Wagner's music, "The Passage of the Holy Grail", portray the Grail as removed from human beholding, to be granted as a vision only to the pure in heart – in practice the true celibates of Arthur's following (Arthur himself never sees the Grail). Hence the Grail leaving the earth symbolises the split between divine/human, its vision promised only to those who renounce earthly (sexual) pleasures – and then only to men. But a feminist re-telling suggests that the Grail's banishment symbolises the loss of reverence for the interconnectedness of creation, the failure to respect bodily wholeness, as well as the failure to acknowledge woman as traditioner and culture-builder.

But the story does not leave us totally without hope that the two worlds can ever be reconciled. First, the death of Arthur brings an imagined reconciliation with Morgaine: "Morgaine," the dying Arthur asks her, "Morgaine, was it all for nothing then, what we did, and all that we tried to do? Why did we fail?"

> It was my own question and I had no answer; but from somewhere, the answer came. "You did not fail, my brother, my love, my child. You held this land in peace for many years, so that the Saxons did not destroy it. You held back the darkness for many generations, until they were civilised men, with learning and music and faith in God, who will fight to save something of the beauty of the times that are past."[21]

Secondly, when Lancelot has thrown Excalibur into the Lake – and at last the Sword is restored to Avalon – Arthur dies, seeing in Morgaine the face of the Goddess. And finally, in Glastonbury itself, where Morgaine finds the Holy Thorn of Avalon growing, she stumbles on the revelation that the Goddess is everywhere in the hearts of all men and women, in Avalon, and everywhere.

3. The challenge of the "Dark Knowing"

This feminist re-telling of the old legend brings us close to discovering the source of the scapegoating of women as evil. Morgan Le Fay – in all her guises within the Arthurian cycles of legends – is witch, sorceress, evil seducer of Arthur, ever plotting the destruction of the Company of the Round Table and disturbing the purity of the Quest for the Grail.

But once she is seen in the specificity of historical and social context, the story presents one example of a tension which has arisen in many different cultures. What, then, is the "Dark Knowing" of Morgaine? What connection – if any – does it have with darkness?

Far from suggesting racist overtones of "black magic" I suggest that the "Knowing" of Morgaine is dark in its depth, and in its pointing to the ambiguity and complexity of living, the interweaving of good and evil, of passion and pain, as part of human experience. It suggests that if we are to be "connected knowers" in any real sense[22] – that the chaotic, messy and irrational aspects of living cannot be swept under the carpet. Complex choices have to be faced – where each choice involves some loss of so-called innocence.

Secondly, Morgaine's knowing holds in tension the tragic and the creative life-giving dimensions of life. It challenges an over-rational, ordered existence, recalling us continually to the participation of feeling and emotion with rational decision-making, and the need for an ethics which takes all these dimensions into account. Thirdly, she also recalls us to ancient, sacred values, long forgotten: Christianity is at last waking up to the ecological crisis and trying painfully to regain connectedness with the earth. Its foundational doctrines of creation and redemption are beginning to embrace concern for the wellbeing of the whole planet. Thus categories of human sinfulness must now include the rejection of a destructive humano-centrism, which has over-focused on humanity at the expense of the environment, legitimising the "rape of the earth".

The challenge of the "Dark Knowing" of Morgaine is, finally, the deliberate integration of bodily, sexual and erotic feeling as part of our growth processes: that which has been degraded, despised and spiritualised away by Christian theology has to be reclaimed as life-affirming, healing energy. And this is the very source of the scapegoating of women as evil. Once we have lost touch with a view of life which held together the oppositions of body/spirit and reason/emotion, and preferred a vision of goodness as pure, unembodied Spirit, separate from all that is material, women inevitably became the symbol of the despised carnality, the messy chaos of bodily emotions and processes, which *homo spiritualis* must shun. Perfection became the attainment of transcendence, seen as the transcendence of the physical and sexual. Thus "Dark Knowing" is a metaphor for holding on to the wholeness and connectedness which may be the only hope of saving our planet.

The magnitude of the ethical challenge needs to be grasped.

We are not being asked to reject inherited wisdom – where this is sound – nor to relapse into paganism, exchanging our post-enlightenment rationalism for the price of a few magic spells and potions. Revelation as Connectedness – through the prism of the "Dark Knowing" of Morgaine – is above all a call to respect "*difference*", particularly the difference of subjugated groups vis-a-vis dominant powers, and minority communities in their faiths, traditions and values. "Just Connections" are only formed through a long process towards dialogue, never through assimilation and suppression of "otherness". Secondly, the "Dark Knowing" of Morgaine is an invitation to re-connect with the earth's ancient rhythms, in the wisdom of herbal lore (for example, through alternative medicine) with the energy of wind, sun and moon, recognising both destructive and creative dimensions. To attempt to find both meaning and a means to live through tragedy, decay and loss is one of the purposes of all World Faiths. But the point of "Connecting" with seasons and elements is not advocated as a self-indulgent life-style (a kind of "Salvation in the Sauna" approach) but to discern which forms of suffering and evil belong to the natural cycle of birth/death/rebirth, and which are the responsibility of human injustice and exploitation, with awareness of the overlapping of the two categories. Thus it is not death itself which is the problem. When one is "old and full of years" there is a sense of the rightness of earthly life coming to a close. It is untimely death, or painful death through accident, murder, abuse, starvation, poverty, war or one of the diseases caused by contemporary life-style which make us call death "evil" and threaten to rob life itself of any meaning. The suppression of Avalon – like the conquest and suppression of Navaho Indians and Australian aboriginals – hid not only a set of values which respected interconnections, but meant that an impoverished Christianity then lived by **oppositional consciousness** and **false innocence**.

The "oppositional consciousness" of "Either/Or" not "Both/And", characteristic of a philosophy of separation, epitomises this way of thinking, and we can scarcely grasp the way in which human potential has been stunted by separative dualisms. For *homo sapiens* in the West has flourished by glorifying reason over against feeling, the physical and the sexual; consciousness over against the unconscious (the dark feminine) and the world of image and symbol. Virtues such as "will-power", "self-control", "strong-will" are associated with the necessary progress to conscious self-hood of the individual. Seldom is it understood that this exhortation to will-power and "mastery" over ourselves and our warring instincts stems both from a philosophy of separation and from the legacy of St Augustine, Martin Luther and the dominant strand of Christian theology which understood sin predominantly as pride, based on the flawed human will.

"Being in control" also expresses the strongest motivation of the foreign policy of most countries, made empirically manifest by the stock-piling of arms and swift military intervention, to give an example of one area of ethical debate.

Furthermore "innocence", in its general usage, is most often understood as non-involvement. But it has more frequently the sexual connotation of being "untainted", of a lack of sexual knowledge, and is linked with the notion of integrity as meaning lack of sexual experience. *Virgo intacta* is a frequently used symbol of Mary, Mother of Jesus. Thus where false "innocence" is extolled, it encourages a lack of responsible action in the face of world problems. "Withdrawal" from the world in pursuit of self-indulgent holiness is a mis-use of solitude and contemplation.

Yet "innocence" in its Latin origin is not a passive non-involvement but an active "not-injuring", "not inflicting harm". Within a philosophy of connection, I use "innocence" as a metaphor for a life-style which respects earthly rhythms and seeks a way to do so in the context of a variety of apparently conflicting cultures.

"Dark Knowing" within a philosophy and epistemology of connection also seeks to embed the human will in structures of care and connection. Rooted in these structural forms – which respect both carer and cared-for – our will becomes, not a narrow "self-will", but rather a fuelling of relational energy, driving to connect and heal broken connections, to re-connect (thus establishing juster forms of community within a specific context) and not to divide, separate and alienate.

Eros, too, will be restored from its negative valuation as merely a necessary basis for *agape*, or other-centred love. The devaluing of *eros* has assisted in the joyless trivialising of natural processes, body-denying spiritualities, and the glorifying of pain in the pursuit of sanctity. Carter Heyward and Beverley Harrison note the close connection of pain, pleasure and violence in sado-masochistic sexual relationships:

> Because in the system good Christian men and through men's author-
> ity, women as well – must deny the enjoyment of flesh, females,
> darkness, evil, and the sensuality associated with these negativities,
> early Christian anthropology required that pain – the deprivation of
> sensual pleasure – be accepted as an important element in attaining
> the joy of salvation.[23]

Heyward and Harrison note that Liberal Christianity has moved from a body-denying Christianity to a qualified embrace of the created world:

> The blatant anti-sensuality bias of the highest forms of patristic and
> mediaeval spirituality has been replaced by the more dialectic dualism
> characteristic of the early Church. Liberal Christianity affirms
> embodied sensuality when it is expressed in heterosexual mono-
> gamous marriage, perceiving that interpersonal intimacy and love
> redeem sex.[24]

Arguing that this is inadequate, these writers claim that *eros* will take on a completely new meaning if sexual energy is given an entirely relational meaning. Thus *eros* is not simply a force which attracts towards "the other", given a limited role in an individu-alist, post-Enlightenment context – in fact built on the split between self and other – but, from the starting point of the "connected self", *eros* become rather the body-mediated energy, enhancing the mutuality of all our relationships, growing "from the soil of non-alienated relationship, as a profound source of an experience of transcendence."[25] It must be emphasized that this definition of the "erotic" has not issued from patriarchal cate-gories but from an enlarged concept of the self. It is akin to the word which Kristeva used to describe female sexual pleasure –

derived from Lacan – as "jouissance". Audre Lord described it like this:

> The erotic provides the power which comes from sharing deeply any pursuit with another person. The sharing of joy, whether physical, emotional, psychic or intellectual, forms a bridge between the sharers which can be a bridge for much of what is not shared between them, and lessens the threat of their difference . . . the erotic functions in the open and fearless underlining of my capacity for joy.[26]

But does Christianity have the resoures for this tremendous exercise of re-imaging *eros* on the basis of connection? Can it face the task of confronting the contexts of human pain and suffering here in an earthly context, without offering merely an otherwordly, eschatological solution? The cost of creating structures of healing for this world's pain is the facing of the ambiguity of the "Dark Knowing" of Morgaine.

What is proposed here is far from being a nostalgic, de-historicised call for a return of the Goddess or a glorification of Avalon as *umbilicus mundi*. "Dark Knowing" here is a metaphor for "dangerous memory" – as used in the work of John Baptist Metz and feminist theologian Sharon Welch.[27] It is the memory of what has been suppressed in the name of an absolutized truth, the vertical transcendence of a masculine God in all the specificity of the struggles of a particular age and culture.

It is of course eminently possible that there were many destructive elements in the culture of Avalon, and a value in the efforts of Arthur to rally the British tribes against the threat of invasion. The words of Morgaine to the dying Arthur convey this wisdom, this "Dark Knowing": "You held back the darkness for many generations, until the Saxons were civilised enough to remember something of the beauty of the past", is how she described his achievement. Her wisdom is in recognizing the partiality, the limitedness of achievement and success, given the ambiguity of the context.

"Dangerous memory" is particularly apt in the case of the denial and suppression of the Great Mother and the values she represents. Christianity has acknowledgedly integrated many themes of the older religions into its rituals – particularly the dying/rising themes of the nature religions, and the cross-cultural theme of the birth of the Child of Promise. But with the denial of the Mother through the demonisation of Morgaine, the enemy of the true Christian Knight, Christianity still rejects the full goodness of the materiality of creation and remains exclusive in its assertion of its own truth. Embracing ambiguity, partiality of solution, the limitation on human possibility and achievement, through this "Dark Knowing" of connectedness comes a new naming of good and evil and a new understanding that in the midst of the horror and tragedy which human beings bring upon themselves and the planet, we are not abandoned: Divine passion for justice, beauty and love are being poured out for us. But we have to take heed: Divine presence is vulnerable. The connections are fragile.

On Being All of a Piece/At Peace

DAPHNE HAMPSON

Upon sitting down to prepare this talk,[1] I found myself considering what it is that is absolutely fundamental to me as a person – and so also to my theological writing. A word floated into my mind: integrity. As I considered further what I wished to say, three concepts came to me: "equality", "autonomy" and "truth". Then it occurred to me that these concepts, which are so crucial to me, all fall naturally under the umbrella of integrity!

I felt suddenly all of a piece! It was a good feeling. (We are told in much feminist thought that it is difficult for women to feel good about themselves – so I noted that I was at peace!) After all the struggle that I have been through, I felt reconciled to the steps which I have taken – out of the Church, and out of Christianity. I could have done none other. I knew myself all of a piece – and therefore at peace.

It has not been easy to have left first the Church, then Christianity behind me. I have often pondered why it should have been I who apparently had to take these steps: I, who for twenty years wanted to be ordained, who gave up history to start studying all over again because I had to study theology, who remained an adamant insider to the Church while one friend after another left religion behind them. Certainly pragmatism has not been my course of action. It has not been lost on me what doors closed for me through my leaving. In the late seventies it was I who went as a delegate to early World Council of Churches consultations on the ordination of women. Now it is my friends who are flown to Australia for a General Assembly! I now watch as others don clerical collars; while it was I who sacrificed time, resources and career prospects in the struggle for the ordination of women at a time when others were little interested.

Nevertheless I am at peace. If I were to be true to myself and to find an integrity, I could not in the last resort have done anything else. Indeed I am inclined to think that, had I been ordained, I should in time have had to leave – and that would have been much more difficult. Now I no longer belong to a body which fails to conform to my ethical values; values which must include feminism. Nor do I try to take on board dogmas which I never did believe or with which I struggled. My religion has come to be one with all else which I take for granted about the way the world is constituted. To be all of a piece is surely all that we can hope for. In the case of one's religion it is indispensable both that it conform to one's ethics and, as far as I am concerned, that it is one with all else that I take to be the case.

I shall therefore speak to these three criteria which I find to be crucial to me: equality, autonomy and truth. I shall argue that, in every case, to hold to the ideal concerned rules out being a Christian. This analysis will form the larger part of what I have to say. However, I shall then proceed to make it clear that in no case is being a religious person affected. It is simply that what I shall call the Christian "myth" becomes untenable. In conclusion this will lead naturally into a consideration as to what it means to be a religious person, within the Western tradition, but free of Christianity. Here I shall suggest that it is in particular paradigms which have been central to feminist thought which will be useful to us as we try to conceptualise what it is that God may be.

The first ethical *a priori* for me, to which any religious position which I may hold must conform, is that of equality. Note that I am here speaking of equality as a prescriptive norm as to what should be, which above all one's religion must not contravene. Equality must always be held to be a given; something from which one then deduces the practical consequences. It is not something for which one should have to argue – if indeed that was possible. The framers of the American Declaration of Independence captured this exactly: "We hold these truths to be self-evident, that all men [we must today say men and women!] are created equal." It is interesting that they put their ethics in theological terms: persons are created equal – it is a given, and given by God. (Thus I should not be prepared to follow a line of reasoning which I have sometimes heard, that at present men and women are not in fact in the world treated as equals, and thus also in religion, while working for change, women must at present put up with not being treated as equals.)

What then does equality entail? I should want to hold that it necessarily entails what I shall call equality of representation, in this case the representation of both sexes. By representation I mean both that women shall be represented (shall actually be present) and also that the representational system of the religion (the symbolism) should not be biased against women. It seems to me that only when there is in both these senses representation, can one see oneself as included (as represented, we may say).

I shall start with two examples of the first of these, the need for the actual representation of women, examples which between them make the point well. Consider the following. On the day that I planned this talk, I heard that Margaret Thatcher had resigned as Prime Minister. I monitored with interest my reactions – the reactions of one who has never voted Conservative. I hated seeing that company of grey-suited men close in on her. I felt myself trapped and angry. My thoughts flashed back to a day ten years ago, shortly after I had left the Church. I was cycling along on my bicycle, when suddenly in a moment of existential freedom it dawned on me that actually I did not have to belong to the Church. This was quite something for one to whom God and the Church had been the central fact of her life since she was a young teenager. I could go out into a world in which a Sex Discrimination Act was in place; indeed in which a woman was Prime Minister! (I had not long before been engaged in compiling a paper arguing that women should be allowed to be deacons – the lowest order in the Church!)

The second example. Some time back while listening to the

radio, I heard that the Archbishop of Canterbury, the Cardinal Archbishop of Westminster, and the Moderator of the Free Church Federal Council had issued a statement on the necessity of British support for Ethiopia. I was deeply annoyed and resentful. Why should these three men (for they had to be men given the positions that they held, in two cases by the laws of their churches, in the third case *de facto*) be making pronouncements in public, as it were on my behalf? Notice that in the first case that, though I might disagree with her policies, it was crucial to me that a woman was present; in the second I was unable to hear what was being said, of which I might have approved, because of who was saying it. Thus representation is a *sine qua non*: it is something which has to be right before I can turn to questions of content.

Given that representation, both in this sense of the necessity that women be represented and in the sense of symbolism, is for me an ethical *a priori*, it would seem to me self-evident that I cannot be Christian. I will however spell this out. Let us look at the matter in relation to the Christian scriptures; for Christians must of necessity refer to the bible, since it reports of the supposed revelation which forms the basis of their faith.[2]

Consider firstly the representation of God (that is to say the question of representation in my second sense of the term). The symbolic representation of God within the Jewish and Christian scriptures consists virtually exclusively of names which are applied only to males in that society. "He" is Lord, King, Judge and Father. Furthermore the way in which the concept of God is shaped clearly suggests that he is male – not to say masculinist! "He" is held to be omnipotent, self-sufficient, jealous of competitors (other potential gods are idols), and free from the need to consult! The female, let alone a feminist value system, goes unrepresented. Now the symbolism of a religion, particularly those symbols used for God, is of its essence.

Consider, secondly, the representation of women in the scriptures. Take Jesus' parables. (For Jesus is often said by Christians to have been free of the sexism otherwise so endemic to biblical culture, and the stories he is reported to have told bring us as close as we are able to come to his view of the world.) Nicola

Slee has provided the following statistics.[3] In Mark's gospel there are eighteen main characters, all of whom are men. In Matthew's there are eighty-five, twelve of whom are women – but ten of these are bridesmaids (!). In Luke's there are 108, nine of whom are women. Moreover the men are depicted in a great variety of roles: they are farmers, merchants, doctors, bridegrooms, priests, rich men etc. By contrast the women can be listed exhaustively as ten bridesmaids, a woman searching for a lost coin, a widow seeking justice and a handful of unspecified wives, mothers and daughters mentioned in general terms.

Nor does the situation improve if we turn from parables to the actual historical figures of women; those women who, of recent years, have been the subject of countless Christian feminist sermons. Take for example Ruth. That she is portrayed as imaginative and courageous is certainly the case. Yet for what is it that she is commended? For having raised children to her dead husband, the primary duty of a woman in that patriarchal society. Indeed she is depicted as entirely dependent on the goodwill of men, even that she and her mother-in-law may eat. Her fate is decided upon in her absence by the men at the town gate. It cannot be said that the story conveys equality. Again, the story of Mary and Martha is frequently lifted up. A woman is spared kitchen duty and allowed to sit at a rabbi's feet. To do useful work in conveying equality however, the picture before us would (for once) have to be that of a man sitting at a woman's feet. But that is of course unthinkable! Let us then not pretend that we have before us examples which portray equality between women and men.

Consider thirdly the representation in the biblical literature of that which is considered "male" and that which is considered "female". The male is unfailingly represented (in relation to the female) as good, powerful, and as having priority. (It is no chance that the metaphors for God are male.) By contrast that which is liable to sin, lacking in power and secondary is assigned a female designation. Thus in the book of Hosea (but also elsewhere) the people of Israel, who go astray, are represented as female, indeed compared to a prostitute; while Jahweh and Hosea who are in the right are represented as male. In the

Christian scriptures the Church is designated female in relation to a male Christ. It is sometimes said, as though this were a gain, that humanity in relation to God is represented by a woman, Mary. But this simply fits the pattern of the female being represented as secondary and as owing obedience to the male: Mary declares "be it unto me according to thy word".

Representation is crucial, fixing in our minds as it does a certain understanding of reality. It should be noted that that this is the case is independent of whether one's interpretation of scripture is conservative or liberal. Within Christianity the scriptures are read and at a subconscious level inform people's minds. The medium, we may say, is the message. Thus it may not essentially help to say that we should pay attention to the message (in the case of Hosea, that of social justice) and forget the metaphors in which it is clothed. The medium (the sexist representation) will willy-nilly have its effect. Indeed, well might we ask how this message about justice should be abstracted (and so applied to the situation of women today) when the very terms in which that message is cast denigrates women?[4] The fact that these scriptures are heard in the context of church or synagogue only makes them the more potent. The images are given sacred legitimation. No exegete stands by to tell us that we should extract the message and forget the imagery. Were they to do so, we should be tempted to ask why, if the message is indeed that of justice and equality, it should be couched in such language?

Christianity (and Judaism), it should be noted, cannot discard this literature. For in the case of either religion (and more particularly in the case of Christianity, in which God is said to have entered history in the person of Jesus Christ), it is believed that these scriptures tell us of a revelation of God. History then becomes part of the substance of the religion. If in a church service mention were made of God, but no reference were made to the supposed revelation in Christ, and the scriptures were not read, that service would not be a Christian one. Christians do not simply hold that God is revealed in all times and places. They believe there to have been a particular revelation, in a particular history – to which reference must then necessarily be made. Christianity cannot lose the Bible.

As one who believes in equality, I do not wish to be part of a religion in which such literature is read. It drives me up the wall. There is no way in which it can be for me a medium through which I perceive God.

How does equality relate to integrity – such that my mind was led from the former to the latter? Equality means in effect the valuing of the integrity of each and every human being. In a religious situation in which equality was not negotiable, there could be no representation of one sex as dominant over the other. Persons would then not be undermined, or feel excluded, in the course of practising their religion.

The second value which I find to be fundamental to my ethics and to which, therefore, my religion cannot stand in contradiction, is that of autonomy. I know from experience that my use of this word is liable to be misunderstood (but I can find none better), so I must explain myself. The etymology of the word autonomy is *auto nomos*, that one is to one's self a law. Autonomy does not then necessarily imply the existence of an isolated self, a connotation which it has apparently come to have. (Indeed I should precisely want to argue that one cannot come into one's own, which it is to be autonomous, unless one is involved in essential relations with others.) The opposite of autonomy is not dependence but heteronomy, namely that that which is other than one's self is a law to one.

Now one might well say that in essence the Women's Movement has been about women coming to have autonomy. Women have ceased to see themselves as secondary persons in relationship to others. They have said that they too count (which is not to say that the other does not). Something is not necessarily to be considered right because advocated by one's boss, husband or any other person. Women have asked themselves who it is that they want to be and what it is that they would do with their lives. They have enabled one another, often for the first time, to dare to be themselves. The fact that "things have always been done a certain way", or that "society believes that a certain relationship between men and women is only right", is not to stand if conscience or self-realisation do not so allow.

There is however a clash, I believe, between Christianity and a rightful human autonomy; a clash which follows from the very nature of the religion. Once one has said that there is a particular revelation of God (and not simply that God is everywhere and always present), then the concept of God which is held is one in which God is seen as being in some way apart from and other than the world. Once one has such a concept of God as separate from the world, then there is always present the possibility of a clash between what is believed to be God's will and what people left to themselves might want to think. Again, if Christians believe, as they do, that God made God's self known in a certain period of history through a certain tradition, then that supposed revelation will become in some sense normative as to what is God's will and therefore right.

Thus take the case of the ordination of women. Both sides, counting themselves Christian, do not simply ask, "What is it that we should think good or just?" They ask, "What it was that Jesus did or said", or "What would be the implications of his words were he to be living now?" There is always a reference not simply to issues of justice and rights (indeed even those in favour of ordaining women have been chary of such language), but to the will of God as it has been made known in history. In the case of conservatives they may also speak of God's will as they believe it to be made known in the natural order of creation. Such a religion demands of us a certain heteronomy; that is to say that we should ask after God's will or the nature of God's revelation. It is not simply for human beings, individually or collectively, to do what they will. This heteronomous stance was exemplified for me in a nutshell when, in a recent discussion on the BBC, someone said that there was no reason why the Anglican communion should not have women bishops, for Genesis should not be read as ruling out female authority(!).

For myself, I find it intolerable that God should be conceived to be the kind of being who should have a will which should take precedence over my own. To have such a God must be worse than so to relate to another human being! Nor would I stand for a religion in which reference had to be made to some ancient patriarchal literature. I remember the impact that it made on me, when writing a paper arguing that women should be made deacons, that it was apparently relevant (both sides were agreed on this) whether Phoebe of Romans 16 was indeed a deacon! What did that say to me as a woman living in the 1970s? It was preposterous. I did not know where I was. But such a stance is intrinsic to Christianity.

Christians can never simply dismiss the text, or say that Jesus was wrong, or, indeed, forget about the text and Jesus. Reference will always be made to what was a past period of history and another age. The most that can be done is to argue that one text should be relativised in the light of a more underlying message (such as that God is love). Or that something was conditioned by that time, and that the implications of God's love for today are something else. Or again that God's message unfolds in history and that God has now made apparent to us that which was not previously apparent (which is offensive, suggesting as it does that God could have let evil persist over millenia).

Such a heteronomous stance, such allowing of something else to determine our will, is surely the undermining of ethics. In ethics, quite independently of any exterior authority, one must think out what one believes to be right. (Thus, that women are to be counted as equals is not a matter to be argued over with reference to what a man may have said hundreds of years ago: it is an *a priori* principle.) To subscribe to exterior authorities, whether the Bible or a supposed revelation of God (even though one should read those things as favourable to one's case) goes against everything which women have believed in recent years about their autonomy and integrity. Women, it will be clear, will be at a particular disadvantage in such a religion, for the past to which reference is made was a patriarchal age in which women were secondary.

It will be evident how autonomy relates to integrity. To be a law to one's self, to take responsibility for one's life, is fundamental to what it means to be a human being. One cannot as an adult abnegate that to another without being a "slave" to them. Of course one may temporarily forgo one's own judgment for the sake of a greater good: when the fire alarm sounds one does what the person in charge says. But to subscribe to a religion which allows that certain things about who one shall be or what one shall do have been decided long ago, or lie with the will of another (God having been defined as other than the self), represents the undermining of oneself as a person. There is no way round this in a religion which is predicated upon revelation.

The third criterion which I find to be non-negotiable, to which therefore my religion must thus conform, is what I shall call truth. In designating truth as a criterion I simply mean that all that I believe to be the case must cohere. I cannot compartment-alize: for example, I cannot hold something to be true "by faith", which I could not otherwise credit. In discussing equality and autonomy, I have spoken of what we may call the need for moral coherence: I am adamant that my religion must conform to what I otherwise believe to be ethical. My religion, as I have said, cannot be allowed to undermine my equality and autonomy as a person. What I wish to consider under the rubric of truth is, rather, the coherence between religion and what one may empirically believe to be the case about the way the world is constituted.

Thus two hundred years after the Enlightenment, at which time within European civilisation the matter became trans-parently clear, I cannot but credit that both history and nature are each a causal nexus. That is to say, there cannot be inter-ventions of God; a God who puts his finger in the pie. Nor can there be unique events (events which are not one of a type), or unique examples in nature (which are not one of a category). Within history events conform to type: we can credit that in the ancient world someone crossed a river because we know there is a possible category crossing rivers. But there cannot be one single resurrection (quite apart from all the other questions which would then be raised about what could happen to the resurrected body), for there are no resurrections. Again, there can be people who are closely in tune with God, so this was surely so also of people in the ancient world. However I cannot credit that there could be one person who had a unique relationship to God (albeit that he was in his other nature fully human as Christians proclaim). Christians who hear this will sometimes try to take refuge in the idea that God can perform "miracles"; but this is not my concept of God. (Of course people may heal through prayer, but then that was the case in the ancient world too.)

Nor is it, so far as I can see, of the least relevance (as people will sometimes propound) that now, through modern physics, we believe the basis of reality to be random. If the basis of reality is random, then it has always been random. That this is the case no more makes it possible for there to be unique examples, in the sense of one-off examples. Of course there is a sense in which every example is unique; each instance of a human being is different. But Christians are not simply claiming of Jesus that he was one human among others as are we all, but that he was related to God in a way in which this is true of no other human being. Christianity in a post-Enlightenment age cannot but be a faith stance. But I am not prepared to say that something can be so by faith which is at odds with and does not fit what I believe through reason.

There are those today, however – and this, it would seem, is notably so within the Christian feminist commmuity – who want to say that they have no belief in the uniqueness of Christ and who yet who call themselves Christians! What sense can that make? I have heard it said that my definition of a Christian as a person who believes in the uniqueness of Christ is a conservative definition. But that is not so. A Christian must, however they may wish to express this, believe Jesus to have been the Christ: that is what it means to be Christian. Christians have never been those who simply proclaimed Jesus' message. Gandhi or an atheist might wish to do that. Christians have always proclaimed not simply Jesus' message, but a message about Jesus. Of course they have not always defined his uniqueness in terms of Chalcedonian orthodoxy. The earliest Christians did not do this. Nor have many of the liberal and radical theological thinkers of the nineteenth and twentieth centuries. But they also (let us take as examples Schleiermacher in the nineteenth century or Bultmann in the twentieth), in some way, spoke of the uniqueness of he who was Jesus. To call oneself Christian while having no belief in Jesus' uniqueness is to take a large step further out; indeed I would say it is to fall off the edge. It is, not least, deceptive.

But furthermore one must ask why one who counts herself a feminist should want to call herself a Christian, if she is not compelled to do so. If one believes that there was indeed a resurrection and holds to this by faith, if one thinks that God has uniquely made God's self manifest through this tradition, then one is bound to confess Jesus as the Christ. If such a person also believes in human equality, he or she will be left with the problems which arise from the maleness of this tradition and its symbolism. But it is a consistent stance. However, to subscribe to Christianity, if one believes it essentially to be a myth, would seem, given its sexism, to be an odd move to make. If it is a myth and not true, let us proclaim it so to be and thankfully jettison it. For Christianity can scarcely be held by a feminist to be a good or helpful myth; it is a highly sexist myth.

The relation of truth to integrity is an interesting one. I am suggesting that if one is to have integrity (or one may say a certain integration in oneself) one must needs be all of a piece. Thus it is crucial to me that I should not hold to a religion in which I should have to believe things to be the case which do not comport with my knowledge of how otherwise the world is. What relation does this have to my feminism? None directly. I do however think that, in as much as one as a feminist has no emotional stake in Christianity being true, one is the more likely to be able to look it straight in the eye and see that it cannot be true. Many men have so much bound up emotionally with their Christian ancestry that it may be harder for them than for a feminist woman to take such a step. For she must look on Christianity at the very least with ambivalence.

I have argued that if one would have it that one's religion be compatible with the criteria of equality, autonomy and truth one cannot be Christian. We should note, however, that what is ruled out is Christianity; that mythical system which has carried Western religious consciousness. There is no reason why, should one so wish, one should not be a religious person *per se*; indeed a religious person who draws on much within the Western tradition which is not specifically tied to the Christian myth. Theology in the West has not simply been predicated upon a supposed revelation; there has also been a tradition of so-called natural theology. I shall then, turning again to the three criteria of equality, autonomy and truth, point to the fact that in each case there is no incompatibility between holding to that criterion and being a religious person. It is the specific nature of Christianity which causes the problem.

Thus there can be no possible incompatibility between holding to human equality and acknowledging that which we may call God. Theism as such is not incompatible with the equal dignity of women as persons. (Indeed one might well say that it is a necessary corollary of being a theistic person, or equally a corollary of the goodness of God, that all persons be acknowledged as equals within a religion!) The problem arises in relation to Christianity, as we have said, because Christians believe there to have been a particular revelation in a past period of history. That history and the symbol system of that patriarchal age then become in some way normative for the religion. If however one has no such concept of revelation, but believes that, whatever God may be, God must stand in the same relationship to all ages, no such problem arises.

If, secondly, God is not conceived to be separate from the self, then there is no way in which there could be a supposed will of God which is other than my own. God in this case will be understood simply to be always and everywhere available, the awareness of God given with the human self, so that God is not thought to be separate from the self but coterminous with, if also more than, the individual self. Again, if there is no revelation in history, then history does not become normative; such that it is suggested that something other should be done than those living in the present would think right. Such a religious position thus in no way clashes with or contravenes human autonomy. (There is of course no reason why, holding such a religious position, we should not draw on past religious insights or theological formulations if we find these to be useful. But the choice as to what it is that we shall pick up is ours.)

Thirdly, such a way of conceiving of God means that what we understand by God will necessarily cohere with all else that we believe to be the case. There could not be some knowledge of God which is separate from the rest of human knowledge. The religious person will wish to say that there is that dimension to all that exists which the atheist will wish to deny. But there will be no question of the religious person believing by faith that which their reason denies. Why one should believe that there is a dimension to reality which we may call God is not something upon which I can enter here.[5] For me it is because prayer is powerful that I believe there to be that which I then name God.

Finally, in conclusion, I should like to suggest that it is some of the paradigms which have been central to feminist thought which may prove to be particularly useful in enabling us to conceive what it is that we may mean by God. I name two. Firstly, feminists have in practice thought a great deal about what it is to be a self-in-relation, though I believe there to be more conceptual work to be undertaken here. Much feminist thought has conceived the person to be essentially relational, rather than a discrete self-enclosed entity, placed in apposition to others. If the reason for being theistic (and not atheistic) is that one finds prayer – or concentrated loving thought – for other persons to be efficacious, then models which allow us to speak of that which moves between persons would seem to be useful in our attempt to conceptualise the nature of God.

Secondly, feminists and others (but I notice that it has been almost exclusively women and that may be significant) have in recent years given consideration to the notion of "attention". By attention is meant that concentrated gaze directed at another, or that listening at depth to another, which allows us in love the better to understand them in all their complexity. Doubtless because of the position which they have occupied in society, women have learnt to watch and to listen. This has stood them in good stead. We are, many of us, highly observant, particularly where personal relations are concerned. If God is something to be discerned in our world, and more particularly in the matrix of human relations, then we shall need to have our antennae out. To be a religious person requires, at the very least, that one be attentive.

I believe then that we need a patient separating-out of human religious awareness from that particular myth called Christianity which has carried and shaped it in the history of the West. We need, I have argued, to discard the myth. It is both no longer tenable and highly detrimental to human relations, biased as it is against women. There is however no necessary reason to cease to be theistic persons. Indeed the jettisoning of an untenable myth may make it the more possible to allow our awareness of God to be central to our everyday lives. Feminism may then well propel us into a revolution in religion the coming of which is long overdue.

Women and Christianity: A Horizon of Hope

URSULA KING

The feminist critique of Christianity can engender much negativity. It certainly presents a tremendous challenge, and particular debates can lead to tension and turmoil in people's lives. Sometimes it seems that both proponents and opponents of feminism overrate the power of feminist ideas in their ability to destroy the Christian faith. The feminist challenge addresses the patriarchal structures and androcentric thought forms of all religions and not only of Christianity, although the critique has gone furthest in the Judaeo-Christian tradition. The encounter of faith and feminism is of utmost importance for the place of religion in the contemporary world, and especially for the place of religion in women's lives, but it is not inappropriate to compare this encounter to other debates which also have had a deep impact on religion and which are still with us.

I am thinking here of the encounter between science and Christianity, and between Marxism and Christianity. If one looks at the history of these debates, one can find strong proponents of the idea that either modern science or Marxist thought, or both, will usher in the end of Christianity, just as some feminists, or their opponents, argue that feminism will bring about the end of Christianity. I think this argument is mistaken, not necessarily because of these historical parallels, but for other more intrinsic reasons. These have to do with the nature of faith as an experien-

tially grounded, existential commitment (rather than a prop-
ositional assent to historically developed doctrines) and the
nature of the socio-historical process by which religious traditions
develop through time.

Whilst others speak of either the radical rejection or the recon-
struction of the Christian tradition, I prefer to speak of its transformation – a transformation which involves that of religion and
consciousness, of self and society. It has been loudly claimed and
strongly argued that Christianity and feminism are incompatible
whereas I maintain that faith and feminism belong together,
for reasons to be explained shortly. Christian women reflect
individually and corporately on their contemporary and historical experience of Christianity and, in so doing, they ask: What
does the Christian faith mean in our lives? Does it give us a
horizon of hope? Is it a ground for strength and empowerment,
a focus for identity, a path, a call to wholeness and holiness?
What does the Christian tradition mean for women who have
found a new critical awareness? How much of the Christian past
is still useable for us? Does conversion to the new "gospel" of
feminism mean that Christianity can no longer offer us some
bread of life, but only stone?

Christianity and feminism: Are they incompatible?

The incompatibility of Christianty and feminism is sometimes
boldly asserted. The particular reasons given may be strong and
convincing, but the particular choice of these particular reasons
is never governed exclusively by logic alone. They include
"reasons of the heart", personal factors of feeling and experience
and many other socio-cultural factors, such as one's family background, upbringing and education, the kind of society one lives
in, and so on. Many arguments are weakened by a universalist
fallacy whereby particular women and men, on the basis of
their particular experience and understanding, come to general
conclusions about all women and men. We must therefore ask

what is being compared when Christianity and feminism are opposed. Specific arguments throw up challenges for intellectual debate and have to be met in detail; yet often one has the impression that both Christianity and feminism are understood in a rather one-dimensional, monolithic way without leaving enough room for the complexity and diversity of long historical processes.

If one takes a wider view by approaching Christianity and feminism from a more comprehensive perspective, one can say that they are compatible if one does not maintain a presentist, monolithic/static or too particularist interpretation of either, as I shall explain. The answer to the question of whether Christianity and feminism are incompatible or not depends on one's understanding of both feminism and Christianity.

Let me explain the three qualifications just mentioned. First, a "presentist" perspective looks at the relationship between Christianity and feminism too much from a present-day perspective, from our current situation, without taking sufficiently into account the historical dimension of the relationship between Christianity and feminism. History is all important, but not only for Christianity – to maintain that is only another version of the uniqueness fallacy in seeing Christianity as uniquely different from all other religions, whereas all religions emerge through and are shaped by historical process. By stressing the importance of history I do not interpret history as a theological category but as a complex developmental process through time. Feminism, too, is mostly seen from a presentist, ahistorical perspective when it is considered as an intellectual and socio-political movement of the last twenty years or so which has nothing to do with religion but is entirely secular.

Religion is often a blind spot in dominant contemporary feminist circles, as can be seen from the content of many Women's Studies courses and publications. Though frequently ignored, there exists a long historical connection between Christianity and the modern Women's Movement through the impact of particular Christian ideas and the contribution of Christian women from different churches, particularly from a nonconformist background, in furthering the cause of women. One only has to think of the Christian women at the 1848 Seneca Falls Declaration or, more importantly, the impact of the Gospel in its prophetic vision of freedom and equality in motivating people to work for social and political change. The deeply held belief of the Judaeo-Christian tradition that all people, women and men, are created in the image of God and are equal, was not only a powerful lever for the development of modern egalitarian democracy but also for the take-off of the modern Women's Movement in the nineteenth century. This is not the place to adduce detailed historical evidence, but it is sufficient to say that increasingly more data are coming to light showing the strong connection between women and religion in past and present, the influence of diverse activities undertaken by women spiritual leaders, preachers or prophets, as well as numerous women who became active in the social and political arena fired by the vision of their faith. Instead of saying that Christianity and feminism are incompatible, I would say that feminism would not have been born were it not for Christianity, though Christianity was not the only parent. If the rationalism of the Enlightenment is considered the father of feminism, then Judaeo-Christianity must certainly be considered its mother.

If the first qualification concerns the importance of the historical dimension over against a too narrowly focused perspective on the present in the debate between Christianity and feminism, the second underlines the internal dynamic and change, the complexity and diversity of both realities over against a static, monolithic view. Both Christianity and feminism exist under many different forms. There is not only historical diversity, but also an internal pluralism which is too often ignored in heated debates. We all know that there are different political orientations among secular feminists. Similarly, there is a diversity of religious orientations among "spiritual" and "metaphysical" feminists and, considering Christian feminists alone, there exists a considerable difference in the attitude of Christian orthodox and evangelical women, for example, towards particular insights of feminism. There is no one kind of feminism nor is there one kind of Christianity. The extraordinary pluralism of contemporary Christianity has been authoritatively documented by David B.

Barrett's *World Christian Encyclopedia* (Oxford, 1982): it lists seven large Christian blocs, 156 major ecclesiastical groups and about 20,800 different Christian denominations worldwide. In the light of this institutional pluralism it is impossible for any one person to speak for Christianity as a whole, or even for one church, because there exists so much diversity within each institution. I do not wish to put forward a totally fragmented and atomistic view of Christianity, where one could never speak of distinctive Christian beliefs and practices which are widely shared; I only want to emphasise the internal plurality and complexity of Christianity which is sometimes forgotten in the debates about faith and feminism. "Post-Christian" feminists can be just as dogmatic in their rejection of Christianity as some Christians are dogmatic in their rejection of feminism. Such fixed attitudes do not help at all in advancing critical debate and understanding.

Christian feminists have, of course, a strong case for radical criticism. There is no doubt that the Christian churches are deeply imbued with a patriarchal and androcentric spirit, visible for all to see in their institutional structures, their all-male leaders and spokesmen who mostly go on ignoring the ever-stronger voices of women. Whilst it has been argued that feminism and Christianity are at heart incompatible (secular and so-called "post-Christian" feminists would agree on this), it has also been maintained that Christian feminists may in fact be today's prophets led by the Spirit, calling the churches to a new vision and a new life. Will the churches respond to this call? Will they have the power and will for the transformation needed for women to become full co-sharers and partners in all Christian activities and institutions? It is impossible at present to answer these questions by appeals to empirical evidence. The outcome to the question of whether Christianity and feminism are incompatible, not in essence or at an abstract level but in practice, will be decided in the future – it could go either way. But if the transformation of Christian institutions did not occur, it would be a tremendous and tragic loss for the churches, as women would turn elsewhere to still their spiritual hunger. The need is great indeed, as is evident from the growing number of Christian women who feel deeply rooted in and enriched by their Christian faith and do not want to abandon it as "post-Christians", but who consider themselves as "post-church" feminists unable to take part in traditional Christian worship because of the invisibility and marginality of women.

As a Christian woman one has to hope and believe that the transformation of Christianity is possible. How else could one continue being a Christian? We must not be timid and faint-hearted, though we know that such hope meets many obstacles and requires much courage and strength. But more than ever before Christian women are participating in the process of creative theological thinking which is not without its effects on the practical life of the churches. For most of Christian history women have been excluded from such thinking for, as in other religions, they had little access to theological education. Here lies the key for understanding the Christian history that was. There is no reason why that particular construction of history should be considered as normative forever when we, that is to say all people and the entire world, have undergone such momentous changes.

Such changes often begin in almost imperceptible disguises. As for the theological education of women, it was first asked for in the mid-nineteenth century when, during the first wave of feminism, women began to work for full political and social equality. A few colleges of the free churches then admitted women to study theology, but only with reluctance. Most of the well-known theological schools and universities did not admit women students for another century. The history of women's theological education, which would be mainly a history of their exclusion, still needs to be written, but we know that the access of women to theology in any substantial numbers, allowing for some few exceptions, mostly post-dates the Second World War – in Europe, in North America, and in the rest of the world. Women have become theologically literate for the first time in history. As in other disciplines, women first conformed to and adopted the dominant patterns of thought, eager to follow their masters on well-established paths in interpreting scripture and tradition. But women soon discovered a great dissonance – their own invisibility and oppression throughout much of the formative and normative parts of Christian history and theology. Feminist thought gave women a new sense of identity and independence; it empowered women in theology to develop their own thoughts differently, voice their own speech and proclaim their own vision of faith.

Feminist theology was born. Without women's theological education it would never have come about. This new birth may still be at the fledgling state or perhaps just entering its early youth, but from all one can observe it shows no sign of being a stillbirth. On the contrary, it shows evidence of great vitality and promise, of a tremendous potential to transform Christian life and witness. What began almost imperceptibly a hundred years ago has taken on its own momentum and produced a new theological dynamic whose ultimate effect on the transformation of Christianity, as it is at present known, is impossible to foretell with certainty.

My third point in discussing the relationship between Christianity and feminism concerns the critique of a particularistic or too individualistic a perspective in assessing this relationship. It is perhaps too much to expect that individual women, who for whatever reasons have made a strong personal commitment by rejecting Christianity, will not judge the compatibility of Christianity and feminism exclusively on the basis of their own limited experience. They find it difficult to consider it within a much more comprehensive and global framework. Some of the objections to Christianity remain too Eurocentric and Western, and are not valid globally. Christian women elsewhere in the world, particularly in many parts of the so-called "Third World", are developing their own theological resources and critique, less addressed to the limited theological formulations of Western, Latin Christianity than to the practical aspects of Christian ethics and spirituality. Overall conclusions about the compatibility or incompatibility of feminism and Christianity cannot be derived from a particularist interpretation of Christianity, but have to be based on the strength and witness of Christian faith within a global context. It is in the "Third World" that Christian feminist thinking often provides a powerful inspiration and motivation for women's work in the churches. It is here that the remarkable transformation and reshaping of traditional institutional structures sometimes progresses more rapidly than within the long established, powerful and ossified religious institutions of the West.

Lastly, I would like to argue that the question about the compatibility or otherwise of Christianity and feminism is itself rather too particularistic. Within a more global perspective of theological thinking and religious practice – taking note of the spiritual needs and wellbeing of the entire human community, as well as noting that of the comparative study of different religious traditions – the question about the effect of feminism is much larger than its challenge to Christianity. We do not only have to consider whether feminism and Christianity are compatible, but rather whether religion and feminism are compatible. Radical feminists have answered this question in the negative, again by existential commitment rather than by explicit reasoning and argument. But the case for and against has yet to be adequately argued. This is not the place to do so, for it would lead into a long analysis of the place of religion and spirituality in contemporary society and culture, which has to await another occasion. Instead, I shall conclude with some personal reflections which explain why I see grounds for hope when considering the relationship between women and the Christian faith. This, by the way, seems to me a more appropriate way of speaking. It is not falsely objectified systems such as "feminism" and "Christianity" which encounter each other, but individually transformed women and groups of women whose feminist consciousness has emerged and so changed them that nothing remains unaffected – whether it is their self-understanding and personal identity, their relationships, their faith and the theology derived from it, or their membership and participation in the life of the churches.

Grounds for hope

Following the principles explained earlier, I am well aware that I cannot speak for all Christian women or for any Christian institution. I can only share my own reflections and insights for consideration by others, fully aware that I speak as an individual woman, but with an awareness of the many interconnections between myself and others, and of the great variety of experiences and different situations of both women and men around the world. This includes in particular an acute sense of the differentiated layers of awareness, forms of consciousness and spiritual insight among different members of the human community.

I am less interested in arguing about feminism and Christianity in the abstract than I am concerned with concrete, empirical evidence. Pragmatically speaking, Christian feminism works – there are many Christian feminists for whom their faith and feminism have come together and transformed each other. To maintain, contrary to this evidence, that Christianity and feminism are absolutely incompatible would simply be untrue. Feminism works for some Christian women whilst it destroys the faith of others. I think this has much to do with one's own understanding and practice of that faith in the first place, and also with one's own particular experiences and personality. The diversity of reactions is an indication not of the essential incompatibility of faith and feminism, but of the complexity and what I call the "problematic of ambivalence" of both.

Much has been made in feminist theoretical discussions of the philosophy of interconnectedness and relationality, of the logic of inclusion rather than exclusion, and of the elucidation of other ideas. What has not been explored at a theoretical level is the significance of ambivalence present in most human experiences, symbols, images and ideas. There is ambivalence in every religious tradition with regard to the understanding and description of women. Most religions seem to possess a double typology of women with both positive or negative connotations. Whilst there is a certain dominant overall orientation, there is nonetheless considerable ambivalence of ideas and images, just as there is considerable ambivalence in feminist self-descriptions today. Such ambivalence always requires interpretation, which involves an act of will in deciding which connotation to accept as the most appropriate. In relation to Christianity this means that it depends on the choices of Christian women of faith as to which strands of the tradition they decide to accept as affirmative and empowering for themselves. Through such acts of negotiation, reinterpretation, balancing out and integration a truly creative relationship can be developed between faith and feminism.

Like other Christian women I stand by the Christian faith as a source of confirmation and strength in spite of all the critique and negativity of Christianity in its historical and contemporary forms. The Christian faith has shaped and nourished me, given support and sustenance, especially in times of trial. I do not need or wish to reject it, but only want to see it transformed and grow larger and truer to its own message. The Christian message means for me that suffering and death are linked to growth, life and resurrection, that the transformative power of the living Spirit is always amongst us, and that the mystery of life is linked to the unfathomable power of love.

What one loves most one knows best. One can also criticise it most sharply, but such criticism is most effective when coming from the inside. Then it can produce changes which no outside criticism could. As several feminist theologians have pointed out, Christian feminists not only have the negative task of critique, but also the positive task of constructing Christian theology and life anew. There is a challenge here for women not to give up.

The Christian tradition is extraordinarily rich in symbolic, conceptual and experiential resources on which women can draw more easily and freely today than ever before. To give some Christian examples about the idea of interrelatedness, so much praised and explored by contemporary women: there is the belief in the people of God, in the communion of saints – a community of spiritual connections beyond present life and death. Then there is the central mystery of celebration, thanksgiving and adoration in the Eucharist as the bread of life which we break and take together, shared not only in communion in the church, but quite literally in the labours and rewards of our daily life through the joys and sufferings we experience together. Then there is the mystery of the Church as the body of Christ, a mystical reality with ecclesial, social and cosmic dimensions. None of these are specifically and exclusively for women, yet they are fully inclusive and I can identify with them as sustaining and strengthening for me and other women.

Yet there is more. There is the rich heritage of women saints and mystics, a heritage for all, but of special significance for women. The great "women of spirit" of past and present, women teachers, leaders and guides, provide examplary models of inspiration and strength for women of faith today. I have written at some length about this theme in my book *Women and Spirituality – Voices of Protest and Promise* (London, 1989, 1993[2]) and cannot elaborate further on this here. But it is worth mentioning in this context that women of faith everywhere, from many different religious traditions, are beginning to listen to each other and to the witness of each tradition together. They are experiencing similar doubts and trials in relating their newly found feminist consciousness to the traditional understanding of their faith. Christian women, in their attitudes to feminism, must therefore also take into account the rebound effect which interfaith encounter and dialogue among women will have on the understanding of Christian faith. This opens yet another horizon for women of faith which gives us strong grounds for hope regarding the compatibility of Christianity and feminism.

At the theological level the question of women's inter-faith dialogue is just beginning to appear on the agenda, whereas in more established areas of theological work such as exegesis, systematic or practical theology, hermeneutics, ethics or spirituality, a considerable body of feminist theological work has already appeared. Its variety and richness shows a creativity among women which is truly amazing. Such richness is not only evident in North America, but now also in Europe and other parts of the world. It was very much on my mind here in Britain as this essay was being written during the preparation of the Fourth European Conference of Women in Theological Research, organised at the beginning of September 1991 at the University of Bristol. Its theme "Liberating Women: New Theological Directions" indicates both the dynamic of forward movement and the quest for new theological answers – new answers which women need and for which Christian women are working. The fact that there are so many Christian women doing this – the conference counted over 150 participants from all parts of Europe – is another ground for hope.

The feminist critique of Christianity can be acrimonious and deeply painful. It can be shattering in its effect on some Christian women, especially young ones who may experience a sense of loss, confusion and utter disorientation. I sometimes wonder what the ex-Christian feminists who reject Christianity so vehemently wish to achieve? Or what is the aim of those Christians who, equally vehemently and no less dogmatically, reject feminism and insist on the letter of Christianity but not its spirit? Such a dogmatic stance on either side can only lead to an impasse and stagnation, not to a way forward. I think it is important not to come to rash conclusions nor to proclaim them in too shrill a manner. What is needed is a cautious and careful assessment of the arguments on all sides, but also a realistic appraisal of the speed and scale of transformation currently occurring in women's minds and hearts. Intellectual and existential faithfulness to our Christian tradition is important – and many women show such faithfulness to a high degree – but we also need all powers of discernment to recognise the signs of the spirit working among us in the world and the churches today. The new spirit among women can give Christians great ground for hope.

NOTES

Chapter 1

1. Ludwig Wittgenstein, *The Blue and the Brown Books* (Oxford, Basil Blackwell 1958), p.57.
2. Mary Daly, *Beyond God the Father* (Boston, Beacon Press 1973), p.19.
3. Cited from Elizabeth Clark, *Women in the Early Church* (Wilmington, Michael Glazier 1983), p.35.
4. Cited from Arlene Swidler, "The image of woman in a father-oriented religion" in *God as Father?*, ed. J.-B. Metz and E. Schillebeeckx, *Concilium*, 1981, p.75.
5. Rosemary Radford Ruether, "The feminine nature of God: a problem in contemporary religious life" in Metz and Schillebeeckx, *ibid.*, p.63.
6. John Chrysostom, Homily XXIII.
7. Cited from N. Kemp-Smith, ed. *David Hume: Dialogues Concerning Natural Religion* (Indianapolis, Bobbs-Merrill 1947), p.10.
8. Sallie McFague, *Models of God* (Philadelphia, Fortress Press 1987), pp.18–19.
9. Ruether, *loc. cit*, p.66.
10. Dorothee Solle, "Paternalistic religion as experienced by women" in Metz and Schillebeeckx, *op. cit.*, p.73.
11. Paul Ricoeur, "Fatherhood: from phantasm to symbol" in D. Ihde, ed., *The Conflict of Interpretations* (Evanston, Northwestern University Press 1974), p.468.
12. "Representation" in this (Hegelian) sense Ricoeur defines as "the shaped (*figurée*) form of the self-manifestation of the absolute". *Ibid.*, p.481.
13. *Ibid.*, p.482.
14. Robert Hamerton-Kelly, "God the Father in the Bible and

in the experience of Jesus: the state of the question", in
Metz and Schillebeeckx, *op. cit.*, pp.96, 98.

15. *Ibid.*, p.97.

16. Ricoeur, *op. cit.*, p.486.

17. *Ibid.*, p.487.

18. *Ibid.*, p.489.

19. Hamerton-Kelly, *op. cit.*, p.100.

20. The degree of intimacy implied by the title *Abba* has
     recently been questioned, but even if it is not equivalent to
     the modern "daddy" the argument above holds. It still, as
     Barr points out, belongs to the familiar and colloquial regis-
     ter of language. Nor need it be of crucial significance
     whether Jesus was first to address God as *Abba*. That he
     addressed God so at all would still be an eschatological
     marker. See James Barr, "Abba Isn't 'Daddy'", *J.T.S.*, N.S.
     39, 1988.

21. Ricoeur, *op. cit.*, pp.490–1.

22. Ricoeur, *op. cit.*, p.479. In discussing the explicitly Christian
     reading of texts, including texts of the Hebrew Bible, Rico-
     eur is not thereby saying the Christian reading is the only
     or best reading of them. Obviously Jews read the same
     texts quite differently, and without the Christian teleology.

23. *Ibid.*, p.497.

24. I should emphasize that the use of "father" as a Messianic
     title in the New Testament does not oblige one to give a
     central role to the title in contemporary religious practice,
     especially in situations where its use might convey the
     opposite of hope and promise. It is one messianic title
     amongst many and needs to be understood in its literary
     and historical context, but even so understood it may need
     to be used with caution. Those who do not see why the
     "father" title should be problematic for women might well
     read the chilling indictment by Susan Brooks Thistlethwaite
     in her *Sex, Race, and God*. Writing on the basis of work
     with battered and sexually abused women, Thistlethwaite
     recognises that the original intent of the "father" title was
     not to justify violence against women but says, "For me, in
     my work with these survivors, it does not fundamentally

matter. The entire history of Western abuse of children, particularly of girl children by fathers, stands between us and those texts; and no amount of ahistoricism can change that fact" (p.114). Thistlethwaite also notes, however, that black Christian feminists in America do not have the same difficulty with "father" language as do white feminists and that a certain amount of toleration is needed with regard to preferred divine titles.

25. Jurgen Moltmann, "The Motherly Father. Is Trinitarian Patripassianism replaing theological patriarchalism?" in Metz and Schillebeeckx, p.51. I have some difficulties with Moltmann's ascription of literal usage to the second but this is not to the point here.

26. *Ibid.*, p.52.

27. *Ibid.*, p.53.

28. Julia Kristeva, *In the Beginning Was Love: Psychoanalysis and Faith* (New York/Guilford, Columbia University Press 1987), p.32.

Chapter 2

1. *Modern Theology*, vol.2, no.3, April 1986, p.238.

2. Alwyn Marriage, *Live-Giving Spirit* (London, SPCK 1989), p.54.

3. *Ibid.*, p.45.

4. Leonardo Boff, *The Maternal Face of God* (London, Collins 1989), p.93.

5. *Ibid.*, pp.116f.

6. Sarah Coakley, "God as Trinity: an approach through prayer", in *We Believe in God* (London, Church House Publishing 1987), p.120.

7. Jurgen Moltmann, *The Crucified God* (London, SCM 1974), pp.241, 243.

8. *Ibid.*, p.244.

9. William Oddie, *What Will Happen to God?* (London, SPCK 1984), p.112.

10. There is a story of a Downside monk visiting a mental

institution. He was taken to meet a new patient who believed himself to be the Holy Spirit. In a fit of frivolity, the monk asked the patient, "Can you tell me the answer to a question that has vexed the Church for centuries: do you proceed from the Father alone, or from the Father and the Son?" The patient drew himself up and replied, "We *never* talk shop". This is perhaps the best resolution of the problem that I have heard.

11. Ephesians 4:13.

12. It was noted in discussion after this paper had been delivered in Cambridge that, while I express considerable reserve about the current Trinitarian formula, "Father, Son and Holy Spirit", I continue to use it throughout the paper. I do indeed have reservations about its usefulness, but I cannot find any satisfactory alternative. There have, of course, been suggestions in the past: Augustine, for example, puts forward "Memory, Intellect and Will". But, as he himself immediately goes on to note (*de Trinitate*), each of these terms could be applied to any member of the Trinity, and this is the case with all alternative Trinitarian formulae. The point is that the members of the Trinity are not differentiated to us by function, but by their relations to each other, and this is hard to capture any better than is done by "Father, Son and Holy Spirit", even if this is not wholly satisfactory.

Chapter 3

1. The translations from Genesis have been made by the author. It should be noted that in the transliterations from the Hebrew the silent aleph and aiyin have not been transliterated.

2. **adam**: The word is usually translated as "man". As we shall see (p.51), the word is derived from a feminine noun, *adamah*, meaning "ground". In order to heighten the sense of adam (not Adam) as the singular form of humanity, I shall leave the word untranslated throughout.

3. "**the** adam". The text uses the expressions "adam" and "**the** adam" – *ha'adam* הָאָדָם – interchangeably. The use of the direct article, "the" – *ha* ה – emphasises the fact that *adam* is not a proper name. The word only becomes a proper name in Genesis chapter 3, when it is used to identify the man as distinct from the woman, who does not receive a name until "adam" gives her one (3:20 – Ḥavvah חוה , from the root ḤYH, חיה to *live*), thus establishing his authority over her (one of God's punishments for the eating of the tree of knowledge – 3:16).

4. The most common term for God in the Hebrew Bible is Elohim – a masculine plural of the noun El אל, suggesting diversity in unity, which is mirrored by the diversity in unity of humanity: *adam*, *zachar* and *nekeivah*.

5. According to Jewish tradition, the consonants YHVH יהוה are to be translated as "the Lord". This follows the vocalisation of the Hebrew text: the consonants YHVH are supplied with the vowels of the word *Adonai* אד־ני , literally, "my Lords". As related in Leviticus chapter 16, the consonants YHVH representing the Ineffable Name of God, were only pronounced by the High Priest in the Holy of Holies of the Temple on the Day of Atonement. Since the Temple was destroyed in 70 CE – and the Priesthood along with it – the true "sound" of the consonants has been lost. Since YHVH seems to be connected etymologically to the root HYH היה, to be, I have followed one traditional liturgical practice of translating these letters as "the Eternal". That the biblical writers drew a conscious connection between YHVH and the root HYH is evident in the account of the "burning bush". When Moses asks for God's **name**, so that he can tell the Israelites enslaved in Egypt who has sent him (Exodus 3:13), God replies: "*Ehyeh asher Ehyeh* אהיה אשר אהיה"; "I am/shall be that I am/shall be . . . Thus shall you say to the Israelites: Ehyeh has sent me to you" (3:14).

6. Etymologically speaking, the words *'ishah* אשה and *'ish* איש probably derive from the root, 'NSh אנש – although the *yud* – in *'ish* is problematic (the *dagesh* –

"point" – in the *shin* שׁ of *'ishah* represents the missing *nun* נ). The plurals are *nashim* נשׁים (f), and *'anash-im* אנשׁים (m), respectively. Interestingly, the standard dictionary of the Hebrew Bible, Brown-Driver-Briggs, making reference to Arabic parallels, identifies **two** such roots: one meaning "to be inclined to be friendly, social" – from which *'ish* is derived; one meaning to be soft, delicate – connected to the separate root, 'NSh אנשׁ, to be weak, sick, from which *'ishah* is derived (pp.60–1). However, apart from the irregularity of the yud in *'ish*, there is no logical reason for seeing the two words, *'ishah* and *'ish*, as being derived from separate roots.

Chapter 4

1. See, for example, Simone de Beauvoir, *The Second Sex* (Penguin 1972), pp.679–87; Mary Daly, *Beyond God the Father* (London, The Women's Press 1968), pp.98–131; Beverly Wildung Harrison, "The Power of Anger in the Work of Love: Christian Ethics for Women and Other Strangers" in Ann Loades (ed.), *Feminist Theology: A Reader* (London, SPCK 1990), pp.194–213. Don Cupitt, consciously employing a feminist approach, gives a similar analysis of Christian ethics in *The New Christian Ethics* (London, SCM 1988).

2. The description is K.K. Ruthven's from his book *Feminist Literary Studies* (Cambridge University Press 1984), p.35.

3. Andrea Dworkin, *Our Blood* (London 1982), pp.61–2.

4. Virginia Woolf, *Three Guineas* (New York, Harvest/HBJ 1966).

5. Such a critique has already been applied with great profit by several women working in the field of feminist theology. I have in mind here the work of someone like Angela West who, in her interpretations of Paul, has been able to show that he is not the arch-enemy of all women, as he has been made out to be. In the process she has revealed just how much many of his male commentators have missed, how much meaning they have suppressed, ignored, or distorted.

See, for example, A. West, "Sex and Salvation: A Christian Feminist Bible Study on 1 Corinthians 6:12–7:23", in Ann Loades (ed.), *op. cit.*, pp.72–80.

6. I do not think that the claim that there is no such thing as a Christian ethic – a claim which cites as evidence the supposed disagreement of those who talk about Christian ethics – is substantial enough to merit attention here. A good response is given by Gordon Graham in *The Idea of Christian Charity* (University of Notre Dame Press 1990), pp.71–73.

7. The case for these assertions is made by Oliver O'Donovan in *Resurrection and Moral Order* (Leicester, Inter-Varsity Press 1986), ch.11.

8. I am thinking here not so much of the work of a particular writer as of a conception of morality which is common in our society, albeit often unspoken and unexamined. John Rawls gives perhaps the clearest and most systematic statement of this moralty in *A Theory of Justice* (Oxford University Press 1973).

9. See also, Dorothy Dinnerstein, *The Rocking of the Cradle and the Ruling of the World* (London, Souvenir Press 1978) and Jean Baker Miller, *Toward a New Psychology of Women* (Boston, Beacon Press 1976).

10. Carol Gilligan, *In a Different Voice: Psychological Theory and Women's Development* (Harvard University Press 1982), p.26.

11. *Ibid.*, p.28.

12. *Ibid.*

13. Simone Weil, *The Need for Roots* (London, Routledge and Kegan Paul 1978), p.3.

14. Helen Oppenheimer, *Law and Love* (London, The Faith Press 1962), p.29.

15. *Ibid.*, p.29.

16. *Ibid.*, p.28.

17. See, for example, Carol Gilligan, *In a Different Voice*; Marianne Garbrucker, *There's a Good Girl* (London, The Women's Press 1988); and Sue Cox, *Female Psychology: The Emerging Self* (Science Research Associates 1976).

18. Irving Singer documents several of these in *The Nature of*

Love, Vol.3: The Modern World (University of Chicago Press 1987).

19. Anders Nygren, *Agape and Eros* (One-volume edition: SPCK 1953).

20. Most notably in chapter 12 of Helen Oppenheimer, *The Hope of Happiness* (London, SCM 1983), pp.101–123.

21. *Ibid.*, p.114

22. Mary Daly, *Pure Lust* (London, The Women's Press 1984), p.360.

23. *Ibid.*, pp.362–386.

24. Oppenheimer, *The Hope of Happiness*, p.184.

25. Quoted by E.O. Springstead in *Simone Weil and the Suffering of Love* (Cambridge, Mass., Cowley 1986), pp.80–81.

26. See, for example, Daphne Hampson, *Theology and Feminism* (Oxford, Basil Blackwell 1990), pp.121–26. Hampson quotes Niebuhr saying that sacrificial love is "a moral norm relevant to interpersonal (particularly family) relations, and significant for parents (particularly mothers, heroes and saints)". (*ibid.*, p.126). See also Ann Loades, *Searching for Lost Coins: Explorations in Christianity and Feminism* (London, SPCK 1987), pp.39–60.

27. Ann Oakley, *Taking it Like a Woman* (London, Fontana 1985), p.54.

28. Soren Kierkegaard, *Works of Love* (Princeton University Press 1946), p.73.

29. Oppenheimer, *The Hope of Happiness*, p.107.

30. *Ibid.*, p.120.

31. *Ibid.*, pp.125–26.

32. Murdoch writes, "I have used the word 'attention', which I borrow from Simone Weil, to express the idea of a just and loving gaze directed upon an individual reality. I believe this to be the characteristic and proper mark of the active moral agent." Iris Murdoch, *The Sovereignty of Good* (London, Routlege and Kegan Paul 1970), p.34.

33. Oppenheimer of course qualifies her belief that persons can legitimately worship one another, and excludes idolatrous forms of relationship. See *The Hope of Happiness*, pp.140–46.

34. Augustine, *Confessions*, IV, 10.

35. One of the most interesting calls to take maternal love seriously – on a philosophical rather than a theological plane – is Sara Ruddick's *Maternal Thinking: Towards a Politics of Peace* (London, The Women's Press 1990).
36. The words are C.S. Lewis's from *The Four Loves*, p.152.
37. Quoted by O. O'Donovan, p.240.
38. Quoted by O. O'Donovan, *ibid.*, p.239.
39. Daphne Hampson, *op. cit.*, pp.121–26.
40. Oppenheimer, *The Hope of Happiness*, pp.102–103.
41. *Ibid.*, p.103.
42. Andrea Dworkin, *Intercourse*, (Arrow 1988), pp.198–99.

Chapter 5

1. The distinction between biology and culture, or nature and nurture, is very frequently used in discussions of sexual differentiation. My distinction does not entirely correspond with that, and will be further elaborated later in this paper.
2. See Christina Dodwell, *In Papua New Guinea* (London, Pan 1985).
3. I am indebted to Nicholas Denyer, who heard the talk in question, for this example and for many other helpful ideas and comments, including the title.
4. See, for instance, Leslie M. Lothstein, *Female to Male Transsexualism*, (London, Routledge & Kegan Paul 1983); also M. Eber, "Gender Identity Conflicts in Male Transsexualism", *Bulletin of the Menninger Clinic* 44 (1980) pp.31–38; M. Eber, "Primary Transsexualism: A Critique of a Theory", *Bulletin of the Menninger Clinic* 46 (1980) pp.168–82; E. Person and L. Ovesey, "The Transsexual Syndrome in Males: I. Primary Transsexualism", *American Journal of Psychotherapy* 28 (1974) pp.4–20; E. Person and L. Ovesey, "The Transsexual Syndrome in Males: II. Secondary Transsexualism", *American Journal of Psychotherapy* 28 (1974) pp.174–93.
5. See N. Chodorow, *The Reproduction of Mothering* (Berkeley and London, University of California Press 1978).

Chapter 6

1. L. Boff, *The Maternal Face of God* (London, Collins 1989).

2. A.M. Jaggar, *Feminist Politics and Human Nature* (Brighton, Harvester 1983), and R. Tong, *Feminist Thought – A Comprehensive Introduction* (London, Unwin Hyman 1989). As will be clear, I am greatly indebted to the accounts of these two authors in what follows, and I acknowledge their influence gratefully.

3. Republished more recently: Betty Friedan, *The Feminine Mystique* (New York, Dell 1974).

4. C.G. Heilbrun, *Toward the Promise of Androgyny* (New York, Knopf 1973), my emphasis; cited in Tong, *op. cit.*, p.31.

5. R. R. Ruether, *Sexism and Godtalk* (London, SCM 1983), pp.153, 154. The tone of the Mariological discussion in this book is somewhat different from Ruether's earlier *Mary – The Feminine Face of the Church* (Philadelphia, Westminster Press 1977), in which the stereotypical language of "femininity" is used on the whole uncritically – at least until the final section (pp.79f.).

6. M. Daly, *Beyond God the Father* (Boston, Beacon Press 1973), p.84.

7. *Ibid.*, p.140.

8. B.C. Pope, "Immaculate and Powerful: The Marian Revival in the Nineteenth Century", in C.W. Atkinson, C.H. Buchanan and M.R. Miles, eds., *Immaculate and Powerful: The Female in Sacral Image and Social Reality* (Boston, Beacon Press 1985); see pp.174, 192.

9. S. Firestone, *The Dialectic of Sex* (New York, William Morrow 1970).

10. See M. Daly, *Gyn/Ecology* (London, Women's Press 1979), pp.107–312.

11. A.M. Jaggar, *op. cit.*, p.88. The discussion that follows here owes much to Jaggar's illuminating chapter 5.

12. Quoted by Jaggar, without precise reference, *ibid.*, p.88.

13. M. Daly, "The qualitative leap beyond patriarchal religion", *Quest* vol.1, no.4 (Spring 1975), pp.30–1.

14. See especially J. Alpert, "MotherRight: A New Feminist

Theory", *Ms* (August, 1973); A. Rich, *Of Woman Born* (New York, W.W. Norton 1976); S. Griffin, *Woman and Nature: The Roaring Inside Her* (New York, Harper 1980).

15. M. Daly, *Gyn/Ecology*, p.194.

16. M. Warner, *Alone of All Her Sex* (London, Weidenfeld and Nicolson 1976), p.159.

17. *Ibid.*, p.339.

18. M. Daly, *Gyn/Ecology*, p.87; for "male femininity", see p.85.

19. M. Daly, *Pure Lust* (London, The Women's Press 1984), p.74.

20. M. Daly, *Gyn/Ecology*, p.231.

21. *Ibid.*, p.88.

22. *Ibid.*

23. M. Daly, *Pure Lust*, p.128.

24. C. Weedon, *Feminist Practice and Post-Structuralist Theory* (Oxford, Basil Blackwell 1987), p.135, my emphasis.

25. I am drawing especially on T. Moi, ed., *The Kristeva Reader* (Oxford, Basil Blackwell 1986); E. Marks and I. de Courtivron, eds., *New French Feminisms* (Brighton, Harvester 1981); and J. Kristeva, *Desire in Language: A Semiotic Approach to Literature and Art* (Oxford, Basil Blackwell 1980). The secondary exposition in Weedon, *op. cit.*, and T. Moi, *Sexual/Textual Politics* (London, Methuen 1985), I have found very helpful.

26. J. Kristeva, *About Chinese Women* (London, Boyars 1977), p.16; cited in T. Moi, *Sexual/Textual Politics*, p.165.

27. In T. Moi, ed., *The Kristeva Reader*, ch.7.

28. In Kristeva, *Desire in Language*, ch.8.

29. T. Moi, *The Kristeva Reader*, p.180.

30. *Ibid.*, p.175.

31. *Ibid.*, p.183.

32. See Kristeva, *Desire in Language*, p.249.

33. T. Moi, *The Kristeva Reader*, p.180.

34. See J. Gallop, *Feminism and Psychoanalysis: The Daughter's Seduction* (London, Macmillan 1982).

35. Jaggar, *op. cit.*, chs.6 and 10; also see Tong, *op. cit.*, ch.6.

36. Jaggar, *op. cit.*, p.315, my emphasis.

37. R.R. Ruether, *Sexism and Godtalk*, p.155.

38. *Ibid.*, my emphasis.

39. *Ibid.*, p.158.

40. I. Gebara and M.C. Bingemer, *Mary, Mother of God, Mother of the Poor* (London, Burns & Oates 1989).

41. *Ibid.*, p.14.

42. *Ibid.*, p.161.

43. From the cover of the British edition.

44. See John Paul II, *Mulieris Dignitatem* (London, Catholic Truth Society 1988). There are some striking similarities of theme and approach.

45. See *ibid.*, p.68.

46. Boff, *op. cit.*, p.42.

47. *Ibid.*, p.38.

48. Even then, Boff's citation of de Beauvoir (see, e.g., p.41) suggests a strange and partial reading.

49. See Boff, *ibid.*, pp.238ff.

50. C.G. Jung, *Collected Works* 9, II, p.14; cited in N. Goldenberg, "Jung After Feminism", in R. Gross, ed., *Beyond Androcentrism* (Missoula, Montana, A.A.R. 1977), p.57.

51. *Ibid.*, pp.53–66. Goldenberg concludes her analysis of Jung's theory of the self thus: "On a practical level the anima/animus model and its goal of unification works better for men than for women. The model supports stereotyped notions of what 'masculine' and 'feminine' are by adding mystification to guard against change on the social sphere where women are at a huge disadvantage. In practice, men can keep control of all 'logos' activities and appropriate just whatever 'eros' they need from their women as a kind of psychological hobby. Women, on the other hand, are by no means as encouraged to develop 'logos', since they are thought of as handicapped by nature in all 'logos' areas such as those found at the top of any important profession" (*ibid.*, p.60).

52. Boff, *op. cit.*, p.79.

53. *Ibid.*, p.13.

54. *Ibid.*, p.77.

55. *Ibid.*, p.254.

56. *Ibid.*, p.249.

57. *Ibid.*, p.103.

58. See S. Coakley, "'Femininity' and the Holy Spirit" in M. Furlong, ed., *Mirror to the Church* (London, SPCK 1988), pp.124–35.

59. Boff, *op. cit.*, p.189, my emphasis.

60. It is a nice irony that just such a recent philosophical theorizing of motherhood (from a secular feminist writer, Sara Ruddick), concludes that the highest maternal virtues are those of "humility" and "attentiveness" (see S. Ruddick, "Maternal Thinking", in J. Trebilcott, ed., *Mothering: Essays in Feminist Theory* (Totowa, New Jersey, Rowman and Allanheld 1984), ch.13; and, more fully, in S. Ruddick, *Maternal Thinking* (Boston, Beacon Press 1989)). Ruddick's tough-minded analysis of the epistemology and ethics of parenting, whilst owing nothing conscious to Mariological traditions, nonetheless returns unwittingly to central Marian themes. So realistically are they reworked, however, as to point at least one hopeful way forward for an authentically feminist philosophy of motherhood. The contrast with Boff could scarcely be more marked.

Chapter 7

1. See Nel Noddings, *Women and Evil* (Berkeley, Ca., University of California Press 1989), ch.1, pp.5–34.

2. I have discussed this problem in "Augustine and the Legacy of Guilt", *New Blackfriars*, Vol.70, No.832 (Nov. 1989), pp.476–88.

3. Elaine Pagels, *Adam, Eve and the Serpent* (London, Weidenfeld and Nicholson 1988).

4. C.S. Lewis, *A Grief Observed* (London, Faber & Faber 1961), p.50.

5. Dorothee Soelle, *Suffering* (Philadelphia, Fortress Press 1975), p.32.

6. See Nel Noddings, *op. cit.*, ch.2, pp.35–58.

7. This point is made with great effect by Demaris Wehr,

Jung and Feminism: Liberating Archetypes (London, Routledge 1988).

8. The tensions are evident in contemporary Jewish feminist struggles to uncover Goddess traditions as conflict *within* and not against Judaism. See Judith Plaskow, *Standing Again at Sinai* (San Francisco, Harper and Row 1990).

9. Amid the proliferating literature on the Arthurian cycle of legends I have chosen Marian Zimmer Bradley's *The Mists of Avalon* (London, Michael Joseph 1982), because of its specific attempt to de-patriarchalize the myths. Also to be noted in this respect should be Fay Sampson's retelling of the different stages of Morgaine's life, for example *Wise Woman Telling* (London, Headline 1989).

10. Glastonbury has acquired new prominence today as a centre of "New Age Spirituality" and the Gaia Movement.

11. Monica Sjoo and Barbara Mor, *The Great Cosmic Mother*, (San Francisco, Harper and Row 1987).

12. *Bede's Ecclesiastical History* (London, Dent 1910), Bk.3, ch.2.

13. Tacitus, *Agricola*, (London, Penguin Classics 1948), p.80.

14. R.J. Stewart, ed., *Merlin and Woman* (London, Blandford Press 1988), p.171.

15. Marian Zimmer Bradley, *The Mists of Avalon, op. cit.*, p.13.

16. *Ibid.*, p.15.

17. Early sources include Sir Thomas Malory, *La Morte d'Arthur* (London, Headline 1961); Wolfram von Eschenbach, *Parsifal*, (London, Penguin 1980) Geoffrey of Monmouth, *History of the Kings of Britain* (London, Penguin 1966); Chretien de Troyes, *Arthurian Romances* (London, Dent 1987). For a contemporary study see John Matthews, ed., *The Household of the Grail* (Wellingborough, Aquarian Press 1990).

18. Dolores Ashcroft-Nowicki, "Merlin and the Mother Goddess", in Stewart, *op. cit.*, p.171.

19. *Ibid.*, p.168.

20. Zimmer Bradley, *op. cit.*, p.888.

21. *Ibid.*, p.1000.

22. See, for the theme of "connected knowing", Mary Field Belenky *et al.*, eds., *Women's Ways of Knowing* (Basic Books 1986); Mary Grey, "Claiming Power-in-Relation: Explor-

ing the Ethics of Connection", *Journal of Feminist Studies in Religion*, vol.7, no.1 (Spring 1991), pp.7–18.

23. Carter Heyward and Beverley Harrison, "Pain and Pleasure: Avoiding the Confusion of Christian Tradition in Feminist Theory", in *Christianity, Patriarchy and Abuse*, Joanne Carlson Brown and Carole S. Bohn, eds. (New York, Pilgrim 1989), pp.148–173.

24. *Ibid.*, p.159.

25. *Ibid.*, p.166.

26. Audre Lord, *Sister Outsider: Essays and Speeches* (Trumansberg, New York, The Crossing Press 1984), pp.56–57. For an attempt to develop a new theology of Eros, see Carter Heyward, *Touching our Strength: The Erotic as Power and Love of God* (San Francisco, Harper and Row 1989).

27. See Sharon Welch, *Communities of Resistance and Solidarity* (New York, Orbis 1985); *A Feminist Ethic of Risk* (Minneapolis, Fortress 1989).

Chapter 8

1. This article is based on my talk given in Cambridge on 3rd December 1990 in the "Women's Voices in Religion 1990" series.

2. My *Theology and Feminism* (Oxford, Basil Blackwell 1990), particularly chapters 2 and 3, considers these questions of language and symbolism in detail.

3. Nicola Slee, "Parables and Women's Experience", *The Modern Churchman*, 26, no.2 (1984), pp.20–31.

4. I owe this point to a student of mine, James Sandbach.

5. My forthcoming book, *After Christianity*, will discuss this.